new studies of old villains

ALSO BY PAUL VERHAEGHE

On Being Normal and Other Disorders: A Manual for Clinical Psychodiagnostics

Beyond Gender: From Subject to Drive

Does the Woman Exist?: From Freud's Hysteric to Lacan's Feminine

Love in a Time of Loneliness

new studies of old villains

A Radical Reconsideration of the Oedipus Complex

PAUL VERHAEGHE

Foreword by Juliet Mitchell

OTHER PRESS · NEW YORK

Production Editor: Yvonne E. Cárdenas
Book design: Natalya Balnova

This book was set in 11.4 pt Bembo by Alpha Design & Composition of Pittsfield, New Hampshire.

10 9 8 7 6 5 4 3 2 1

 Printed in the United States of America on acid-free paper. For information write to Other Press LLC, 2 Park Avenue, 24th Floor, New York, NY 10016. Or visit our Web site: www.otherpress.com

Library of Congress Cataloging-in-Publication Data
Verhaeghe, Paul.
New studies of old villains : a radical reconsideration of the oedipus complex / Paul Verhaeghe ; with a foreword by Juliet Mitchell.
p. cm.
Includes bibliographical references and index.
ISBN 978-1-59051-282-1
1. Oedipus complex. I. Title.
BF175.5.O33V47 2008
150.19'52—dc22

2008031790

contents

foreword

It is difficult to "introduce" Paul Verhaeghe's brief but elegant argument—his book is an immensely accessible introduction to some very difficult ideas and introducing it is liable to add to rather than detract from the complexities at stake. Of course in saying this what I may be confessing to is the fact that certainly I myself have a less tenacious grasp on the topic than the author—this is undoubtedly the case!

Paul Verhaeghe points to the primary problem of sexuality: sexual tension is unbearable and must be discharged; simultaneously, sexual tension is the acme of pleasure and such ultimate joy must be risked. Verhaeghe sees Freud's notion of an Oedipus complex as an unsatisfactory and specifically hysterical resolution of this impossible contradiction. Lacan's "return to Freud" eventually offers a new postulate, a Lacanian coinage to express several ideas at once: the "sinthome." Toward the book's conclusion, Paul Verhaeghe explains the sinthome as something different from the neurotic symptom (to which it refers): "through [it] we can both resolve and simultaneously always doubt any solution to the problem—we can only make each 'sinthome' our own, living its particular dualism of fantasy-resolution and rejection. This introduces a new possible understanding of 'gender.'" This contention is extremely interesting and important—I shall return to it below.

Freud introduces the problematic of sexual tension in the *Three Essays on Sexuality* (1905), where he does not mention the Oedipus complex that had appeared earlier, with the publication of *The Interpretation of Dreams* (1900). In support of Verhaeghe's argument here, the Oedipus complex is dreamt in the dreams of hysterical patients and of their then sometimes hysterical analyst—Freud. (It was finding hysteria in himself, a man, that had led to Freud's universalizing it and hence to the importance of the "universal" Oedipus complex.) Oedipus expresses the dilemma as lying between what everyone wants and no one is allowed—incest with the mother—all you want is all that you cannot have. When you displace your incest-bearing mother onto another woman than your mother (your wife) you will be able briefly to enjoy that contradiction in an orgasm that simultaneously expresses the ultimate desire and the prohibition of it—the pain and pleasure of ecstasy. For Verhaeghe, this Freudian account offers a false answer to the problem of untenable tension being the same as "the acme of pleasure." Lacan's explanation places the dilemma elsewhere: the human being is both sexually driven (has a sexual drive) and is utterly helpless (the prematurity of our birth necessitates our prolonged infantile dependence). We desire the very person from whom we are most in danger—our mother.

Neither Freud nor Lacan could rest content with their solutions, but their different explanations (some of which Verhaeghe considers better than others) leave the fundamental problem, if not untouched, then as, perhaps, what it must be—irresolvable at a general human level.

The Oedipus complex gave Freud the benefit of discovering a therapy—psychoanalysis—that would solve the problem of unbearable/ecstatic pleasure displaced not only onto the wife but also into areas where it goes wrong—neurotic symptoms, inversion, perversions, deviations. These can be put back on the oedipal track where they can be treated. However, Verhaeghe shows that although Freud never abandons the Oedipus as the shibboleth of psychoanalytic theory and treatment, it clearly also never quite satisfies him.

Explaining Freud's false solution to the problem of sexual tension as an hysterical one enables Verhaeghe eloquently to debunk our cherished myths: it is not that there are authoritarian fathers who must prohibit our incestuous yearnings, it is that we also dream up and adore these fabricated monsters. Sylvia Plath's "every woman adores a fascist" is the universal hysterical solution, part and parcel of the false answer of the Oedipus complex. Freud retained but moved on from such hysterical imaginings to propose the conflictual life and death drives. The life-drive subsumes sexuality. The innate "death-drive" drives the organism to reduce all tension and return to a state of inertia, while the opposing innate "life-drive" increases tension by building and seeking ever-new unities. The contradiction of sexual tension is thus an inevitable outcome of these two opposed biological forces.

For Verhaeghe, in offering the life and death drives Freud may address the fundamental dilemma of pleasurable/unbearable sexual tension, but he is then guilty of a new biologism. However, I do not believe this quite ends Freud's search, as he returns to it in his last complete work—the very flawed but fascinating "three essays" of *Moses and Monotheism* (1938), with its emphasis on trauma and social and individual "prehistory"—pre-Oedipus.

Verhaeghe challenges Freud from different directions—using Freud's own doubts against the explanations he had proffered and reinforcing these by calling on contemporary observation, clinical doubts, and various diverse psychoanalytical positions such as Object Relations, Attachment, and Relational theory. As a reader, one finds that each time one engages with, disagrees, or endorses a perspective, Verhaeghe shifts ground until one realizes that no single position will do. Each simply contributes to a fundamental critique of any as-yet proffered solution to the fundamental problem.

Lacan's work interrupts but does not deflect the search for an explanation. Initially he places the focus not on the infant's incestuous love for the mother but on its need for the "fascist" father to protect it from its mother's devouring "crocodile" (prehistoric) love. This is a different view, but as an explanation it is still within the oedipal/castrating terrain and fails, according to Verhaeghe's account, properly to confront the question of the contradictory flow of sexual tension. Lacan later rephrased his explanation: because of human helplessness/dependency, the life-drive's *jouissance* (ecstatic enjoyment/orgasm/use of another) can only be experienced through the other/Mother. This Mother/other seduces the infant by caring for it (as Freud also noted). This, however, as far as I can see, only substitutes a pre-oedipal for an oedipal explanation: savior fascist fathers are replaced by femme fatale mothers. The problem of sexual tension is not resolved.

Verhaeghe favors Lacan's final efforts in his coinage of "*le sinthome*." All the symptoms that result from the Oedipus complex, whether Oedipus is a problem or a solution, are inevitably the provenance of mankind (*Saint homme*) about which one must doubt (Saint Thomas) what is, or is not, real (Christ's wounds/transubstantiation, consubstantiation). We fantasize the perfect fascist father and femme fatale mother but we must also see them for what they really are—bigger, more powerful, sexually desirous. We must identify both with our own particular fantasies and with our own particular doubting (our individual sinthomes), and from this satisfying/doubting position live out our different versions of the contradictory nature of the drives and of the tension of sexuality. We are helplessly dependent upon someone who is, and must be, as lacking as we are and therefore as rapaciously desiring. Caught up in this too is the fact that the identification we must each make will be with our own particular, individual version of gender—a suggestion that Verhaeghe claims changes our understanding of gender.

Both Paul Verhaeghe and I have puzzled about gender through the lens of psychoanalysis for many a long year. In this book, although Paul leaves the question open, he has nevertheless taken a look down a new vista. I'm not sure exactly what he has seen but it would seem to have to do with gender as individually constructed. If this is so then it would range from the utopian normative to an imaginative but perhaps psychotic blip, something that has always fascinated me in one of Robert Stollers's transsexual boys, John, who claims that he knows the difference between the sexes is marked by the penis but that he likes to think that everyone is different—"as snowflakes are different." (Stoller, 1976) As indeed each snowflake is crystographically distinct, this is a wonderful image for what is at stake. I have argued (Mitchell, 2008) that lateral relations of "gender" may be more individual than "sexual difference," which has to do with reproduction, but even here there are two classifications—girls and boys. The classification of gender is not the same as the symbolism of sexual difference and does not so strenuously challenge the analogy to the crystallographic uniqueness of each snowflake—John is refusing a rule rather than foreclosing on the way humans live.

To continue what I feel is a dialogue with Paul, let me suggest that we use the woman, not the man, as the model with which we can explore the problem of sexual tension. The jury is out on the gendering of pre-oedipal infancy. My own position is that, although there are culturally variable behavioral/emotional differences, I would not consider—so as far as psychoanalysis and its object in researching unconscious processes are concerned—that in infancy there is a substantive difference between genders: both experience both while they learn to sort them out. In looking at the question, then, from the woman's side, I am considering this perspective of the woman as available to both sexes. This suggestion may not produce an answer but it does, I think, change the playing field.

In *The Three Essays*, as Paul says, Freud confronts the problem of sexual tension. He considers various explanations, finally debunking the favored contemporary idea that it is the buildup of superabundant semen that causes the painful aspect of the need for discharge. Freud rejects this on the grounds that such a thesis does not account for tension in "infants, castrated men—and women." What is missing from our accounts, I think, is the way the psychic structures that later (post puberty) fall to the woman-side of "sexual difference" are present for both sexes in infancy. We know why and how a little girl is phallic; but not how a little boy is vaginal, or how the specifically female genitals are uterine. That, according to Freud, these female sexual organs are "not discovered" until puberty does not mean they are not there—the actuality of the "real" here should cast a doubt on the fantasies that exclude it. Why, too, is the clitoris not specifically female for both genders rather than only a shrunken penis? His parents question Little Hans on his reaction to his newborn sister: "Why do you laugh?" "Because her 'widdler' is so lovely," he replies.

Boys, like girls, have insides into which food disappears and from which feces proceed; so too in the imagination are there babies—Melanie Klein was surely correct here in saying that infants imagine something puts them in and then they come out. Unlike Klein, I would suggest that at least the older infant's reproductive fantasies are parthenogenic—but the important point here is that they are neither more nor less the provenance of girls than of boys. If we read these fantasies through their deferred meaning to the point when fertility ensues in puberty, then I suggest we get another scenario than the castration complex as regulator of sexuality and representative of death.

Freud notoriously persisted in his statement that death was not directly represented in the unconscious—that castration stood for it. Pontalis (1981) was one of the most emphatic to argue against this position. Here I will only point out that if we take "woman," not "man," as our point of reference, then sex and death come together in a different way because death as a result of sex is a reality for women. This also offers another way with which we might regard the enigma of sexual tension. Realistically, giving birth endangers the life of the mother, still all too often physically and always psychologically—after it, she is not who she was before. The danger of death haunts every possible mother. In infancy every boy and girl is a possible mother, giving birth in fantasy, on the knife edge of procreation and annihilation. This will be realized with the transformations of puberty. Freud gestures toward this in essays like "The Three Caskets" and continues till the end to point out that psychoanalysis, like biology, finds that it is death that is brought into play with the advent of sexed reproduction. There is no death with asexual reproduction such as cloning. "Sexed" death's representational expression is contained in passive copulation, pregnancy, and parturition. If sex is death, tension in orgasm is likely.

Juliet Mitchell
University of Cambridge

Notes

Mitchell, J. 2007. "Procreative Mothers and Childfree Sisters." In *The Future of Gender*, edited by Jude Browne. Cambridge, UK: Cambridge University Press.

Pontalis, J-B. 1981. "On death-work." In *Frontiers of Psycho-Analysis*. London: Hogarth Press.

Stoller, R. 1976. *The Transsexual Experiment*. London: Hogarth Press.

preface

The aim of this book is easy to define: I want to present both Freud's and Lacan's theories on the Oedipus complex. I have limited my study to these two authors—although limited is not exactly a good word here—for a very simple reason: they are the two authors that I know best. I could add that, in my opinion, Freud is not studied enough today—even in psychoanalytic circles themselves. And of course, Lacan is notoriously difficult and important at the same time, making an investigation of his work in this respect worthwhile. The results of my study can be summarized in two short paragraphs—but I'll need the whole book to explain them.

First of all, both in Freud and in Lacan, we find a theory on the Oedipus complex that can be understood as a scientific theory of defense that endorses and supports the (basically masculine) oedipal fantasies and anxieties. The installation of the incest prohibition and—more generally—the limitations on sexuality and sexual pleasure are not the result of this Oedipus complex, they are its very aim. That is, the aim of the typically neurotic, even hysterical subject.

Secondly, to discard both Freud's and Lacan's oedipal theories because they are wrong is a too hasty reaction, one that will be all the more hasty because it confirms a contemporary doxa: that Freud is wrong anyway. As I will demonstrate, beyond this theory lies another one that is more difficult, asking for a totally different understanding. In Freud, we find only the outlines, summarized in his new drive theory: Eros versus Thanatos. Lacan goes further; he even goes so far as to discard Freud's oedipal theory and—moreover—his own "return to Freud," at least in this respect. His new conceptualization reduces the roles of the mother and the father to mere pawns in a larger interplay between society and the drives.

The remarkable thing is that the post-Freudian era finds a perfect mirror in the contemporary post-Lacanian era, because in both cases the focus is almost exclusively on the first part of their theories, if only to refute them. It can be said that we meet here with a triple duplicity. Society—Lacan's "social cunning"—installs a certain role distribution between the parents and the child; the neurotic fantasy of the hysterical subject uses this distribution in order to cope with the individual's own anxieties concerning sexuality and the drive; and psychoanalytic theory followed this in a certain way, by developing an oedipal theory that underscores the neurotic fantasies and anxieties.

The idea that postmodernism and feminism have solved this problem is naive. In fact, the major change they have brought to it is yet another form of social cunning, a reshuffling of the roles with a promise of jouissance for the coalition of the willing. The thing is that the supposedly willing are not so willing after all . . .

new studies of old villains

introduction

The notion of the Oedipus complex regularly pops up in public discourse these days, often in a simplified or caricatured form. A little girl will fall in love with daddy, sparking her envy of mommy; vice versa, the little boy will fall in love with mommy, and therefore become envious of his dad. This dialogue between a mafia boss and his analyst in *Analyze This* (1999) offers an amusing example:

> PAUL VITTI: "Why would I want my father to die?"
> DR. BEN SOBEL: "Well, you said that you were fighting.

He slapped you around because you were rebelling against his authority. It may have been some unresolved oedipal conflict."

VITTI: "English, English?!"

DR. SOBEL: "Oedipus was a Greek king who killed his father and married his mother."

VITTI: "Fuckin' Greeks!"

DR. SOBEL: "It's an instinctual developmental drive. The young boy wants to replace his father, so that he can totally possess his mother."

VITTI: "What are you saying, that I wanted to fuck my mother?!"

DR. SOBEL: "No, it's a primal fantasy."

VITTI: "You ever *seen* my mother? Are you out of your fuckin' mind?"

DR. SOBEL: "It's Freud."

VITTI: "Well then, Freud's a sick fuck . . . and you are too for bringin' it up."

Indeed, this caricature shows how Freud's Oedipus complex is a *father* complex, but I will return to that later. While references to the Oedipus complex are prevalent in public discourse and popular culture, current psychoanalytic discourse gives it much less attention, while at the same time maintaining a kind of uncomfortable silence about "the castration complex." Browsing through the work of almost any post-Freudian author, one can notice that the accent has shifted toward the pre-oedipal determinants, with the mother in a key role. In the light of Freud's theory this can be considered as a sort of overcorrection. While Freud focused exclusively on the father, post-Freudians have switched sides, so that nowadays, especially in Anglo-Saxon theory, it is the mothers who prevail.

A similar conclusion can be made from a sociological point of view. In contrast to the conventional idea of family (with the father as the undisputed authority, the mother as the obedient housewife, the children good and neurotic), contemporary fathers have not only lost their authority, they *themselves* are missing. The increase of single-parent families is essentially an increase of fatherless families, where a mother not only takes care of her child(ren) on her own, but also, from time to time, of a (usually temporary) partner.

Based on these two considerations, one might be tempted to link the fading away of attention paid to the Oedipus complex in the theoretical realm on the one hand and the disappearance of the father from Western society on the other, and argue that the contemporary shift in emphasis away from the Oedipus complex is only a reflection of a broader social change. Yet this explanation is at a minimum incomplete, and I would also add incorrect insofar as it ignores the kernel of the matter. As I will explain later, this kernel is situated in the *function* of the oedipal structure rather than in the specific roles of the parental protagonists and their alleged importance, be it mother or father.

These specific roles—and, accordingly, any particular manifestation of the Oedipus complex—are always tied to a particular place and time. This means that every plea for a return to the eternal values of the good old days can be considered as the expression of a conservative reflex. The fact that such an argument in favor of a return can be made under the veil of a psychoanalytical "theory" (Naouri, 2004), is in my understanding a perfect illustration of the most typical solution of the Oedipus complex—that is, a plea for a certain father image. I will argue that this is even the case for Freud's theory and to a large extent also for Lacan's conceptualization. One of the results of this solution is that the original problem becomes unclear.

We have to go beyond this solution in order to find once again the core problem of the oedipal structure: how to combine identity and drive—that is, desire combined with the person's own drive arousal. For the subject, the common solution is to pass the responsibility to someone else, usually to the woman–mother with regard to the jouissance and to the man–father with regard to the prohibition. Again, to a large extent such a solution conceals the underlying problem, which is the acquisition of one's own identity, in combination with the regulation of one's own drive arousal. In a strange complicity with their patients, psychoanalysts and psychoanalytic theory have endorsed this typical neurotic solution.

father

Freud's oedipal theory as a neurotic solution

Delving into Freud's oedipal theory can quickly result in frustration, since Freud never outlined it in any systematic fashion, though he often mentioned it in passing in studies on other topics (particularly Freud, 1978 [1923e, 1924d, 1925j, 1931b]). The term itself—Oedipus complex—appears for the first time in 1910 (Freud, 1978 [1910h]), although the idea had already appeared in 1897 in a letter dated October 15 to Fliess in which Freud discovers some of his own oedipal feelings, and goes on to describe and generalize them. The generalization is published in *The Interpretation of Dreams*: "It is the fate of us all, perhaps, to direct our first sexual impulse towards our mother and our first hatred and our first murderous wish against our father" (Freud, 1978 [1900a], p. 262). A first major clinical illustration ensues when he elaborates on the case material of Dora (1978 [1905e]).

The contemporary reader of this case study does not even need to know Lacan's critique (2006 [1969–70]) in order to see how Freud's stubborn conviction about the correctness of his oedipal interpretations turns this treatment into a failure. It seems so clear to him: Dora is in love with her father and behaves like a jealous spouse by putting herself both in her mother's place and in that of Madame K. (her father's mistress). The only trouble is that she doesn't want to admit it and leaves the treatment prematurely. He fully applies his knowledge in clinical practice in the case study of Little Hans (1978 [1909b]) on which he elaborates in the Wolf Man (1978 [1918b]).

The two latter case studies have become the classic psychoanalytical references for the development of a hysterical phobia, based on the repressed oedipal feelings of the patient. It is interesting to see how, in a certain respect, the Wolf Man presents us with a reversed mirror image when compared to Dora: although he does accept Freud's oedipal interpretations he remains in analysis endlessly, and Freud has to oblige him to stop. As a result, the Wolf Man starts yet another analysis with someone else and remains in analysis more or less for the rest of his life.

Little Hans and big papa

The first major clinical application is to be found in the case study of Little Hans.[1] It couldn't be better: here is a five-year-old son in full-blown oedipal crisis who is observed by his dad, supervised by Freud. The father of psychoanalysis finds his theory fully confirmed. Little Hans is in love with his mama, wants to possess her, even sexually, and therefore harbors death wishes against his rival, his papa. In view of the unequal distribution of power, these death wishes quickly transform into a mortal fear, albeit with the particular oedipal appearance of castration anxiety. The child's repression of his incestuous desires—instead of renouncing them—lays the fundamental ground for a phobia: anxiety about biting horses and an almighty father. During the treatment, little Hans will learn that he had to be afraid of his father because he desired his mother so dearly, but that he needn't be *that* afraid because his father loves him as well and things aren't so bad after all.[2]

---

[1] In 1906, the year after the publication of his *Three Essays on the Theory of Sexuality*, Freud appealed to his followers to supply psychoanalytically inspired observations of children, in order to endorse his theory on infantile sexuality—which is not a very sound methodological starting-point. Graf, one of his Wednesday evening friends, loyally reported on the romping of his first-born. From a certain point on, this report became a case study. Little Herbert/Hans had turned phobic: afraid to leave the house and afraid of horses. Supervised by Freud, Graf hesitatingly took the first steps on the road to analysis with children.

[2] In Freud's own words: "and I then disclosed to him that he was afraid of his father, precisely because he was so fond of his mother. It must be, I told him, that he thought his father was angry with him on that account; but this was not so, his father was fond of him in spite of it, and he might admit everything to him without any fear" (Freud, 1978 [1909b], p. 42).

Yet a close reading of the case study presents us with a totally different picture. Any castration threats come not from the father, but rather the mother. Moreover, it is the mother who from time to time lectures the father, even in the presence of their son who first and foremost loves his father. If we read Freud's explanation—the phobic anxiety expresses the boy's anxiety for the father—together with a classic psychoanalytical-oedipal interpretation of the giraffe fantasy that stands in sharp contrast to Hans's associations, then it is obvious that something is wrong. Things become even stranger if we see that the treatment, although based on a number of wrong interpretations, has obviously been beneficial for the boy.

Central in this first analysis of a child we find a fantasy featuring a giraffe. What is the story? Having entered the bedroom of his parents during the night, Hans produces the following explanation the next morning. "In the night there was a big giraffe in the room and a crumpled one; and the big one called out because I took the crumpled one away from it. Then it stopped calling out; and then I sat down on top of the crumpled one" (Freud, 1978 [1909b], p. 36).

Of course, this is right up the analyst's alley, that is, the analyst Hans's father imagines himself to be. A more classical script could not be imagined. Giving himself the role of father Laius, he straightaway recognizes little Oedipus-Hans taking possession of the crumpled mother giraffe (Jocasta), while the big father giraffe is reduced to the role of screaming observer. On the whole, he adds, the story is a reproduction of an almost daily scene: the little boy joins his mother in bed in the morning, encountering only feeble protests from his father that are invariably rejected by an irritated mother (ibid., pp. 39–40).

Yet in reading Hans's fantasy and the dialogue that follows, it becomes clear that a number of things are not what they are supposed to be. The interpretation of the father, as given above, is at the very least incomplete and probably wrong. Let us first of all listen to the father's interpretations. "That same day his father discovered the solution of the giraffe fantasy." He *discovered* it. The question is where? Sure enough not with Hans, because the dialogue on that page in no way endorses what the finder has found. The interpretation is an aftereffect of an already established, preexisting knowledge, and is given from the position of the master, the authority: "In the train I explained the giraffe phantasy to him . . ."[3]

An interpretation from the master position charges the other with an explanatory knowledge. Nevertheless, combining Lacan's discourse theory (Lacan, 2006 [1969–70]) with one of Freud's important discoveries, we have to assume that such a master position hides an inner division: "The Ego is not master in its own house" (Freud, 1978 [1917a], p. 143). What is the truth of Hans's father as a divided subject? Throughout the case

[3] Freud warns us in this very case study (Freud, 1978 [1909b] pp. 23 and 121) and in several papers about the explanatory style of the analyst that the patient has to find the meaning of his symptoms for himself; the task of the analyst is to open the pathway leading thereto; see *The Future Prospects of Psycho-Analytic Therapy* (1910d), *"Wild" Psycho-Analysis* (1910k), *On Beginning the Treatment* (1913c), and *Remembering, Repeating and Working Through* (1914g). Many years later, in his turn, Lacan warned against "verbalism," that is, the analyst being all too easily seduced by significations; we have to work with and on the signifiers *as produced by the analysand.*

study, this becomes more and more obvious: the man just can't assume the position of the father. He is the one who talks nonsense, in spite of the fact that Hans is defined as the one who produces the *Unsinn* (the family nickname for his phobia). It is also the father who loyally visits *his* mama in Lainz every Sunday, together with his little boy. Without his wife, that is. And when the father asks Hans what he would do if he were papa, the child answers without hesitation that he would take mama along to Lainz (Freud, 1978 [1909b], p. 89). Children have good noses.

This background information demonstrates that the masterly interpretation of the father testifies to his own fantasy, fulfilling his deepest wish. Indeed he would very much like to take the position of the Father of the Law, "the one who has rightful possession of the mother—and in peace, in principle, and is therefore envied and admired by the son" (Lacan, 1993 [1955–56], p. 204). Alas, in everyday life, Hans is not at all afraid of his father; on the contrary, he is afraid of his mother. It is her to whom he would like to give a good beating, not his father (Freud, 1978 [1909b], p. 81). Moreover, this father does not possess the mother "in all tranquility"; on the contrary, their divorce is on the way (see Freud's appendix on the case).

By 1901, with his *Psychopathology of Everyday Life*, Freud had already discovered that, sooner or later, the truth appears through slips of the tongue and the like. In spite of his thoughtful explanations, the father reveals the truth in a spontaneous reaction: "On Sunday, 29th March, I went with Hans to Lainz. I jokingly took leave of my wife at the door with the words "Good-bye, big giraffe!" "Why giraffe?" asked Hans. "Mummy's the big giraffe," I replied, to which Hans rejoined: "Oh yes, and

Hanna's [Hans's sister] the crumpled giraffe, isn't she?" (Freud, 1978 [1909b], pp. 39–40).

Immediately following this reaction by Hans, the father launches into an explanation that contradicts what he has just said. He very patiently explains to little Hans that he (the father) is the big giraffe (long neck naturally equals long penis), that the small crumpled one is the mother (without a penis), and so on. Hans "confirms" this in a typically hysterical style of complicity with the desire of his father—"the hysteric's desire [. . .] is to sustain the desire of the father" (Lacan, 1994 [1964], p. 38)—in a way that stands diametrically opposed to his (i.e., Hans's) first reaction.

Installation of the father and the therapeutic result

If we take Freud's technical invention (free association) seriously, and if we combine this with Lacan's repeated warnings ("Beware of understanding" . . . "Desire has to be taken literally"), it is obvious that the interpretation of the giraffe fantasy does not tally with the way in which Hans experiences his father during the daily reality of his family life. A Lacanian reading might focus on the fact that Hans's surname is . . . Graf, meaning that the choice of the dream element (*Giraf*) is almost a homonym of his patronym. Although important, this detail probably wouldn't have changed much in the interpretations—even if reversed. It endorses the fact that the dream treats the position of the boy within the structure of the family. And, as Juliet Mitchell has pointed out, the presence of the newborn sister is yet another factor that necessitates the questioning of Hans's position (Mitchell, 2003).

As benevolent as the father's intentions may be, he fails in his specific role as a father for Hans. The boy will never receive a satisfying answer to his most important question: "But I belong to you as well?"—that is, to the father (Freud, 1978 [1909b], p. 87). In fact, his role as a father is almost systematically passed over in silence throughout the case study, even in his *own* chicken-or-egg sex education lesson, in which Our Lord seems to be the decision maker. Hans concludes that both men and women can lay eggs and that he too will be able to have children just like a woman (ibid., pp. 85–88). The father denies this and appeals once more to the Almighty as the One who has taken care of the matter in such a way that only women have children, apparently without any male interference whatsoever ("if God did not wish it none would grow inside her"). The absolute limit is reached when Hans finally turns to his mother. From her, he learns that if mama does not want a child, then God Almighty does not want one either (ibid., p. 91).

In this way, Hans is compelled to feel completely at the mercy of his mother's whims, to which apparently even God has to lower His divine head. Freud puts it as follows: "His father must have had something to do with Hanna's birth, for he had declared that Hanna and Hans himself were his children" (ibid., pp. 133–134). He had declared that he'd had "something" to do with it . . . Hans's symptomatic productions involving horses and chariots were interpreted by Lacan as an expression of the child's most central problem: to whom is he tied, to which chariot? The motherly or the fatherly one (Lacan, 1994 [1956–57], pp. 116–117)? For me, this is the crux of the matter.

Throughout the whole case study, Freud reports intervening only once in person. And it is so weighty an intervention that it is really more of a *construction.* "'Long before he [Hans] was in the world', I went on, 'I had known that a little Hans would come who would be so fond of his mother that he would be bound to feel afraid of his father because of it; and I had told his father this'" (Freud, 1978 [1909b], p. 42). Freud is convinced that with this interpretation he has liberated the child from his fear by explaining to him the meaning underlying his phobic-defensive elaboration. It may, however, have worked in a different way than Freud imagined. By considering it in the light of Lacan's description of Hans's problem above, the therapeutic effect may have been due to the fact that Freud *installs* the father in the very position where the child needs him, thus driving a wedge between mother and child and thereby—as we will explain later on—also between Hans and his own jouissance.[4] The strength of Freud's interpretation is that he not only introduced it for Hans, but *also for the father* ("and I had told his father this"). This, in view of the situation, was highly necessary.

The impact of this intervention on Hans can be measured by looking at the position the child afterward explicitly ascribed to Freud, and in the wake of the latter, to the father. "Does the professor talk to God as he can tell all that beforehand?" Later on, when the father, completely at a loss, asks Hans almost desperately what he is afraid of, the little boy answers without hesitation

---

[4] Jouissance is one of Lacan's most notoriously difficult concepts, especially as it evolved during the development of his theory. Essentially, it indicates the limit between a pleasure arising from the drive that can be controlled and one that cannot, thus threatening us (in our imagination) with the loss of our sense of identity.

that he does not know it himself, but that one should ask the professor because he will surely know the answer. He also expresses his hope that when everything is sent to the professor in a letter, his "non-sense" will be over soon (ibid., pp. 42–43, 48, 61). Freud's intervention has delineated for Hans's father the place he should occupy in the family constellation in Hans's imagination. Obviously, the child has heard this very well, even better than the father himself. As we will see later, the fact that Hans's father is—just like any father—unable to take this position, is much less important than the fact that Hans understands the message.

In contrast, before Freud's intervention, the father twice appeared as an *accomplice* in Hans's fantasies, while the Law and prohibition were represented by a policeman. Both fantasies picture misdemeanors carried out *with* the father (entering a forbidden area in a park, breaking a window in a railway carriage); each ends with both of them being punished by the Law (ibid., pp. 39–40).

At the moment of and in response to Freud's intervention, Hans's father denies adamantly that he was ever angry at Hans, and points out that he has never hit him (ibid., p. 42). Hans immediately replies that of course he has been hit by him (even if only while playing) and thus confirms Freud's construction: for him the father *has* to function as an authority. Later, in an analogous discussion, the father denies being angry and Hans replies: "Yes, it *is* true. You're cross. I know you are. It must be true" (ibid., p. 83).

In the aftermath of Freud's intervention, more and more of the knowledge originating with Freud is ascribed to the father.

Two of Hans's expressions in relation to his father are typical in this respect: "You know everything, I didn't know anything" (ibid., p. 90), and "You know better, for certain" (ibid., p. 91). Moreover, it is now possible for Hans to express his anxiety in a clearer form. He is anxious when his father leaves the house, anxious that the man will not come back (ibid., p. 45). In the dialectical progress of the analysis, this can be understood as follows: now that the father has only just been established, Hans cannot afford to lose him.

To put it briefly, what Freud considered to be the given circumstances—the oedipal, strong father figure standing between mother and child in order to prohibit the incestuous desire of the child—is initially what was lacking for little Hans; it is through Freud's intervention that Hans can begin to view his father in this way. In terms of oedipal structure, Hans clearly needs a strong father figure. And his own daddy seems to be able to take on this position only by referring to yet another father with even more authority: "the professor." We will return later to Freud's and even Lacan's insistence on the existence of an ultimate authority, namely the primal father, from whom every father inherits his power.

Now it could very well be possible that Hans's family is an exception to a general rule and that Freud—since he got the information only secondhand—was mistaken and took his expectations for reality. Nevertheless, when we turn to Freud's other case studies we are in for a surprise. Beginning with the *Studies on Hysteria* (1895d), we meet with weak, ill fathers who need to be taken care of, often enough by the person who later becomes Freud's patient. Lacan talks about "fathers-out-ofcommission" and illustrates with Dora how the hysterical patient presents an idealized father (Lacan, 2006 [1969–70], p. 95). At the time of Seminar XVII, Lacan is already leaving the collision between Freudian psychoanalytic theory and neurotic fantasy concerning the almighty father. The hysterical subject needs to rescue the wounded father, and Freud's oedipal theory helped with the construction of the idealized father. This is a classic case where neurotic fantasy and theory collide. The hysterical impulse behind this rescue fantasy offers to the subject the additional reward of being the author of the rescue. Later on, we will meet this rescue fantasy in the second edition of Freud's primal myth, with Moses as the rescuer.

The discrepancy between this collision and the actual clinical reality becomes even more apparent in Freud's major case studies. We meet with an impotent father who presents his daughter as an object of exchange for the husband of his mistress (Dora); with a father who is a caricature of an Austrian noncommissioned officer, living on the fortune of his wife for whom he left a beloved but unfortunately poor girl (the Rat Man); a melancholic father who wanders from one spa to another (the Wolf Man). By and large, Hans's father is hardly an exception, although he is possibly one of the best! All this demonstrates how the neurotic's definition of the father entails a gap between the pathetic reality he must contend with and the idealized version of the person who is supposed to protect him against something that he fears and that has to do with the mother.

In Freud's clinical field, then, we find more often than not weak fathers, contrary to what one might expect on the basis of his oedipal theory. Moreover, there is a second difference. Classic

Freudian theory dictates that threats of castration—if they are really uttered—come from the father. However, in clinical practice, as Freud himself says, threats of castration come from the mother more often than from the father (Freud, 1978 [1924d], p. 174). Again, Freud's own practice contradicts his oedipal theory.

Triple duplicity: Fantasy, theory, society

For our study, Freud's clinical applications provide the main entry to his Oedipal theory; they make it clear that his Oedipus complex is first of all a *father* complex, with a central role for the son. His very first reference to the Oedipus tragedy is accompanied by a warning about the fall of the "*potestas patris familias*" of his time (1978 [1900a], p. 207). When the young Lacan (1984 [1938]) discusses *les complexes familiaux* four decades later, he too considers the then-current degradation of the patriarchal imago in the family and society to be the main cause for psychopathology. He even suggests that psychoanalysis arose in response to this very degradation and the crisis that ensues from it (Lacan, ibid.)!

This illustrates our point: the triple duplicity between the classic Freudian oedipal theory, neurotic fantasy, and society. The hysterical subject needs a strong father figure, especially if the real father is a weak character. This necessity may lead to the fantasy of a primal father figure, whose idealized function will be endorsed by the classic theory. For patriarchal society the benefit of such an endorsement is obvious, but how this takes place needs further explanation (see our last chapter).

Hence, ironically enough, Lacan is right. From a certain point of view, Freudian psychoanalysis really did arise from a crisis vis-à-vis the role of the father in the family and may be considered as an attempt to mend this crisis. Using Lacan's discourse theory, Serge André has confirmed this thesis, albeit with an important twist: it is the hysterical subject who needs a master figure, and this need explains how hysteria helped to create psychoanalysis (André, 2000). In his reading, psychoanalytic praxis ought to analyze this necessity for the master figure, instead of endorsing it. Post-Freudian theory, on the contrary, will stress the role of the mother, and—in his later theory—Lacan himself will denounce the Freudian fallacy. Nevertheless, today, in certain conservative parts of French psychoanalysis, a renewed plea for the authoritarian father can be heard (Naouri, 2004).

This denouncement comes quite late in his seminars. Before that, and despite the fact that they wrote at different times, their theories are very similar in this respect. Both of them have developed an oedipal theory that comes down to a plea, even an apology for the father, as the necessary guarantee against a drive-ridden danger that has to do with the mother. The most important difference between them is that, for Freud, the danger originates in the desire *of the child* (as a matter of fact, the desire of the son) for the mother, while for Lacan, it is exactly the other way around. For him, the danger originates *in the mother* who desires her child (as a matter of fact, her son) far too much. This difference aside, their theory is similar in that both of them expect a solution from an almighty father figure. It is precisely this aspect of their theories that I consider to be a therapeutic endorsement (via the theory) of the neurotic answer to an underlying problem. As I will elaborate later, this problem has everything to do with what Lacan understood in his last theory to be the idea of "jouissance."

The myth of the primal horde as a safeguard for the theory

Something doesn't fit. Aside from the fact that Freud's oedipal theory talks about the son almost exclusively and hardly ever about the daughter, his theory does not match the clinical data. Normally, we would expect a readjustment after this kind of confrontation with clinical practice. Strangely enough, Freud will not change his theory accordingly. Even the opposite: he sticks to his theory in such a way as to make it explain why clinical reality may be different from what his theory predicts. He will do this by introducing a new concept (primal phantasy) that he will ground in a self-constructed myth. In this way, theory and myth become intermixed—the one grounding the other and vice versa—and are aimed at providing patients with what they need by convincing them that they had it already.

This reverse movement—adjusing reality to the theory—is elaborated in the case study of the Wolf Man. The family scenario is similar to that of Little Hans. Here as well, we find a weak father. Here as well, castration threats are coming from the mother (Freud, 1978 [1918b], p. 86). And here again Freud states that the anxiety of the patient about his father is the most powerful motive for his neurosis (ibid., p. 32). At this point, though, Freud himself must have felt the discrepancy between theory and practice, as he produces an answer to it. How is it possible that a son is afraid of his father when the everyday reality does not give that much reason for his anxiety?

Freud's answer may come as a surprise. In those cases where the daily reality does not fit the scenario as predicted by the theory—that is, in almost *every* case—a child will appeal to a higher-order reality that is preserved in schematic form in the collective memory of mankind. "Whenever experiences fail to fit in with hereditary schema, they become remodeled in the imagination" (ibid., p. 119). The Oedipus complex, according to Freud, would be the most prominent example of these collective schemes, which are capable of remodeling reality for us. Such a scheme supposedly goes back to a prehistoric reality where castration would have been a fact. The memory of it would be part of a phylogenetic heritage that is present unconsciously in every child (ibid.).

Such a hyper-reality—Freud called it a primal phantasy—is supposed to take the upper hand whenever the daily reality fails, and to determine psychological functioning (Freud, 1978 [1916–17]), p. 371ff; 1978 [1918b], p. 119). So even when the real father is weak the child will be afraid of him and ascribe castration threats to him, although they may actually be coming from the mother.[5]

In his anthropological study *Totem and Taboo* Freud reconstructs the underlying historical reality of the childhood of man. Once upon a time, he imagines, there was a primal horde, dominated by an almighty primal father who forbade his adult sons access to the females—his females. The sons get fed up

5 "In this respect heredity triumphed over accidental experience . . ." and "At this point the boy had to fit into a phylogenetic pattern, and he did so, although his personal experiences may not have agreed with it" (Freud, 1978 [1918b], p. 86).

with this situation and one day they unite, kill the father, and devour him, in order to get access to the females. After the murder, they fall prey to feelings of remorse and guilt, resulting in the establishment of two fundamental taboos: the prohibition against killing the father, in combination with the prohibition against having sex with the mother (Freud, 1978 [1912–13], pp. 141–143). Ever since, these two taboos have been indelibly inscribed in our collective memory, together with the anxiety for the primal father—and this inscription will determine the ultimate oedipal content of every member of the *Homo sapiens* species.

Even though he invented this myth himself, Freud seems convinced that its events really took place sometime between the last two ice ages (Freud, 1985 [1915]). For him, this self-constructed myth has to be true. Yet even for seasoned Freudians questions arise. Why is there no indication of a mother figure in the story? Without one, the installation of an incest prohibition seems a bit strange. Nothing prepares us for the sudden appearance of a sense of guilt after the murder, or explains it. The idea of castration is lacking, something that is particularly strange as it is a centerpiece of his oedipal theory (the father threatens his son with castration). The way in which the tale is stored in the collective memory is not at all clear, nor is the way Freud's patients distort their own oedipal reality (a weak father) based upon this collective memory described.

What is clear is that this myth permits Freud to safeguard his theory, in spite of the contradictory clinical reality. It is precisely because in reality the father of his patient is weak that the position of the father has to be guaranteed. The message that

Freud passes to his analysands via his interpretations—that they are anxious for their almighty father who forbids them access to their mother—*is precisely what they need*. Through the myth of the primal horde he endorses the typically neurotic solution (the authoritarian father) by elevating this solution to a supposedly historical reality. Lévi-Strauss criticized Freud's homemade myth very aptly: "In the one case, the progression is from experience to myths, and from myths to structure. In the other, a myth is invented to explain the facts, in other words, one behaves like the sick man instead of diagnosing him" (Lévi-Strauss, 1969 [1949], p. 492).

The irony is that earlier on Freud had already foreseen this kind of neurotic solution, describing it in a short introduction to Otto Rank's 1908 book *Der Mythus von der Geburt des Helden* (The Myth of the Birth of the Hero). It was published separately as *Family Romances* (Freud, 1978 [1909c]).

Family romances

The opening sentence of this short paper plunges us into the heart of the matter: the relationship between man and parental authority, which is to be understood as *paternal* authority. Freud describes an evolution. Initially, the parents incarnate the sole authority for the child, who has no thought of questioning their power. While growing up, the child will compare his parents with other adults, usually to the disadvantage of the parents. That's when a new kind of fantasy, called "family romance" often emerges. The child imagines that his father and mother are not his real parents (there has been a mixup at birth, perhaps adoption . . .). There is a typical and recurring particularity to this: the "real" (i.e., fantasized) parents are thought to be of a much higher standing. Freud adds that this fantasy is elaborated while the child still has no accurate knowledge of the sexual details of procreation. Once the child has acquired this knowledge to a sufficient degree, the content of the fantasy changes to focus exclusively on the replacement of the father figure. Indeed, there can scarcely be a doubt about motherhood, as opposed to the *pater semper incertus est* (paternity is never sure).

Freud observes that the imagined father, the one of nobler origin and therefore with greater symbolic authority, resembles the real father on all counts except in social standing. In fact, the child does not so much create a substitute for the father but rather puts him on a much higher plane (Freud, 1978 [1909c], p. 214). This substitution can be seen as an expression of a child's longing for that lost period in which he or she did not have to doubt the authority of the father. The fantasy is in essence an attempt to draw out this period a bit longer; it is the expression of an urge to restore the *potestis patris familias*. The child needs a father whose authority is beyond any doubt. When this authority inevitably fails in reality, the child will imagine one who doesn't fail.

The myth of the primal horde is nothing but Freud's version of the family romance, with the very same goal[6]—that of

---

[6] By way of interpretation, we can suggest that Freud elevates his own father here to the almighty figure he needs. This is the interpretation put forward by Lacan concerning certain of Freud's dreams (Lacan, 2006 [1969–70], p. 122ff). Following the same line of reasoning, I can refer to Freud's dreams about Rome. His associations in this respect are very instructive, as they contain the following memory. "I

imagining an authority beyond doubt. Indeed, providing a historical guarantee for the paternal authority would make any doubt about the *potestis patris familias* superfluous. With his self-constructed myth, Freud has produced a cornerstone for his oedipal theory that is analogous to the family romance as constructed by the neurotic subject.

The trouble with this reasoning lies not only in Freud's assumption that people are able to distort their perception of reality in a subjective way (in this case, to perceive a weak father as a threatening authoritarian patriarch). Social psychology is full of empirical research that illustrates this amply. My problem has to do with Freud's insistence on ignoring clinical evidence. According to Freud, the oedipal child is afraid of the father because of a desire for the mother, while clinical experience shows that his patients need such an authoritarian father figure. The paternal figure as defined by Freud within his oedipal theory is not the kernel of the problem for the neurotic subject. On the contrary, he is the dreamt-of solution. The ensuing distribution of the respective positions (father, mother, and child)

---

may have been ten or twelve years old, when my father began to take me with him on his walks and reveal to me in his talk his views upon things in the world we live in [. . . .] 'When I was a young man', he said, 'I went for a walk one Saturday in the streets of your birthplace; I was well dressed, and had a new fur cap on my head. A Christian came up to me and with a single blow knocked off my cap in the mud and shouted: "Jew! Get off the pavement!"' 'And what did you do?' I asked. 'I went into the roadway and picked up my cap', was his quiet reply. This struck me as unheroic conduct on the part of the big, strong man who was holding the little boy by the hand. I contrasted this situation with another which fitted my feelings better: the scene in which Hannibal's father, Hamilcar Barca, made his boy swear before the household altar to take vengeance on the Romans. Ever since that time Hannibal had had a place in my phantasies" (Freud, 1978 [1900a], p. 197). And I would like to add: not only in Freud's phantasies, but also in his theory.

presents the neurotic subject with a safeguarding security. Once such a father figure is installed, the subject is secured and may start another, much more reassuring fight: the fight with a father who is either not enough or too much of a father.[7]

We are left with the following question: Why does the subject need a paternal prohibition that leads him to transform his real father into an almighty figure?

---

[7] A nice historical illustration was presented by Lacan when he replied to some May '68 students who had interrupted his seminar: "*Ce à quoi vous aspirez comme révolutionnaires, c'est à un maître. Vous l'aurez*" (Lacan, 2006 [1969–70], p. 207 [You, revolutionists, are looking for a master. You will find one]).

mother

Moses: Credo quia absurdum

Freud and Lacan will produce different answers to this question, albeit with the same style of neurotic argumentation. According to Freud, the father must prohibit the incestuous desire of the child toward the mother. For Lacan, the prohibition is directed toward the mother, not toward the child. And yet, a kernel of Lacan's line of reasoning can be found in an implicit form in Freud.[1] First of all in one of Freud's books that is infrequently read these days, and secondly in his theory concerning the

Oedipus complex for girls and women—a later addition to his original oedipal theory.

One of Freud's last publications, *Moses and Monotheism: Three Essays* can be considered quite literally to be a sequel to *Totem and Taboo*. The latter ends with the words: "in the beginning was the Deed," meaning that humanity began with parricide and the consecutive installation of patriarchy. The opening sentence of *Moses and Monotheism* can be read as its correcting sequel: "To deprive a people of the man whom they take pride in as the greatest of their sons is not a thing to be gladly or carelessly undertaken, least of all by someone who is himself one of them" (Freud, 1978 [1939a], p. 7).[2] The man Freud is talking about is Moses, but the same deprivation goes for the almighty primal father as well, who is given a much more modest

---

[1] The fundamental affinity between Freud and Lacan, which is a recurrent theme of this book, is of seminal importance for the future of psychoanalytic theory. It illustrates that, far from being idiosyncratic, Lacan has helped unearth in the Freudian corpus a number of ideas that run up against a more conventional reading of Freud, one that is pervasive today both in the United States and in Europe.

[2] *Moses and Monotheism* barely gets any attention nowadays, but provoked much protest and criticism at the time of its publication because of its hypothetical character. Moreover, the text is poorly written, as Freud himself confirmed. The fact that he considered *Totem and Taboo* as the best text he had ever produced makes the comparison with his essay on Moses even more interesting, as the latter brings a new version of the myth that is central in the former. It is this new version that I am interested in. The book itself hypothesizes that Moses was not a Hebrew but a high Egyptian official who supported the introduction of monotheism by the Pharoah Akhenaton. After the death of the latter, the priests returned to polytheism and Moses was rejected. He chose the Hebrews as his people, imparted monotheism to them, and led them out of Egypt. He was killed during a rebellion. Later, a new leader, also called Moses, reinstalled monotheism. The two Moseses were later confused and considered as one. The wish for the return of the murdered Moses resulted in the belief of the return of the Messiah and the story of Christ was a reenactment of the story of Moses.

position here. Indeed, in this book Freud presents us with a new version of his primal horde myth, with the mother and the preoedipal period receiving the attention they need.

As a matter of fact, in the essay on Moses we find a twofold attempt to rewrite the myth, in each case without reaching any definite conclusion (Freud, 1978 [1939a], pp. 80–84, 130–132). While *Totem and Taboo* focused exclusively on the effect of paternal power on the sons, this book adds the effect of patriarchy on the female order, matriarchy. In both attempts to rewrite the original myth, Moses wanders around as a go-between, a mediator between an originally (all too) real primal father on the one hand and on the other a kind of imaginary primal patriarch who almost receives the quality of the symbolic father function.

Moreover, in *Moses and Monotheism* the myth of the primal horde is depicted as developing in stages. In the first period only the primal father and his females appear; there are no mothers and language has hardly developed. In the second period the murder of the primal father occurs and unexpectedly results in the establishment of matriarchy. The third stage gave Freud a lot of trouble. As a transitional phase it contains a strange mixture of matriarchy, mother goddesses, clans of brothers, and an emerging totemism. The fourth and last stage brings the reintroduction of the primal father–patriarch, *thanks to an intermediate figure*: the son. This is done in such a way that the father receives divine status, which is precisely the reason why Freud makes the connection with the onset of patriarchal monotheism. The transition to monotheism takes place through a mediator—Moses, Christ, Mohammed—who will reestablish paternal authority once again.

Moses installs Jahweh, Christ did the same with God-the-Holy-Father, Mohammed installed Allah. These three religions of the book at the same time install a very typical male–female relationship, in which the woman is the character who must be controlled because of her supposedly original badness and propensity toward lust. Both Freud and Lacan will follow at least part of this reasoning. In itself, this is not strange: their patients grew up in this kind of religious discourse and as a consequence, their neuroses would be determined by it. What is strange is that both of them considered this discourse to a certain extent as a correct rendering of actuality, while it can very well be read as the imaginary elaboration of and the defense against a threatening part of the Real, that is, the drive (Freud) or jouissance (Lacan). Only Lacan will move beyond this pitfall, and then only in his last theories. From my point of view, this way of defining femininity is nothing but a masculine projection of the man's own drive united with a defense system against it—at the expense of women.

Before going deeper into this new version of Freud's myth, it is worthwhile to notice that Freud himself discovered the flaw in his own reasoning. The Moses character is only able to install the one and only god because the latter is a representative of the father—but the father receives his authority precisely because of a referral to a paternal deity. This circular reasoning leads Freud to the *credo quia absurdum* of the church fathers (I believe it, because it is absurd) (Freud, 1978 [1939a], p. 118). In this respect, the myth of the primal horde is indeed a founding myth that in an arbitrary way links its power to an original father figure to whom all later fathers may refer, as his representatives. The automatic nature of this reasoning explains why the association between father figure and authority remains a problem. The symbolic function of the father is missed, and the focus is more on power than on authority, that is, on the imaginary father image. Freud must have felt this difference too, as he wrote that: "religion also brought the Jews a far *grander conception of* God, or, as we might put it more modestly, the *conception of a grander* God" (Freud, 1978 [1939a], p. 112, my italics). But he was close, very close, because on the next two pages, he connects humanization to the development of speech and the power of the Symbolic order as such.

Hence, Freud's rewriting of his myth of the primal horde is much more than just a further elaboration. Inherent in it is a radical reversal that is much closer to the clinical experience described in our previous chapter. The father is not the one who should be feared. On the contrary, the son *needs* the father quite explicitly and, if need be, will reinstall him. What it is that causes this necessity seems less obvious. Freud's text is not very clear in this respect, but it seems as if the disappearance of the primal father would unleash a threatening matriarchy, and vice versa. What is implicit in his reasoning is that the mother contains a danger that has to be bridled by the father. If the latter disappears, the son fears he will fall prey to this threatening maternal power. Hence it is precisely the son who (re-)installs the paternal authority.

This reinstallment—the rescue of the father figure—is by no means exceptional in the matrix of all neuroses, for example, hysteria. On the contrary, Lacan considered it to be one of the central desires of the hysterical subject (Lacan, 1994 [1964], p. 38). However, one tends to forget that such a salvation of the father figure is directed *against the mother.* Among Freud's clinical cases, there's little Hans, who creates for himself the phallic father to escape from the big maternal bathtub in which he feels in danger of disappearing. There's Dora, who dreams about a father who saves his children from a burning house, against the (jewel case of the) mother. There's Anna O., who writes stories about a daughter saving her father that end happily with the disappearance of the mother (Verhaeghe, 2000 [1987] , pp. 167–170). In neurosis, then, the mother is associated with a danger that has to be curbed with the help of the father.

This radical reversion concerning the father—from feared character to much-needed buffer—in Freud's revision of his primal horde myth has another radical effect in that it renders castration almost irrelevant. In *Totem and Taboo*, castration was mentioned only as a threat, and in *Moses and Monotheism* Freud has the murdered father regain his power via the son; what room is left for even the idea of castration? Freud's classic reasoning about castration as punishment remains, albeit in a weakened version. Instead of castrating his rebellious sons, the primal father can be just as easily satisfied by throwing them out. More importantly, circumcision—a weakened form of castration—appears as a symbol *for the pact with the founding father-god* (Freud, 1978 [1939a], pp. 26, 44, 122). Castration/circumcision seals the pact with the father? Clearly, it has taken on a different meaning here, and is no longer just a form of punishment. Freud, though, does not make this change explicit. We may consider it to be a precursor of what Lacan will later call *the symbolic castration.*

Lacan's crocodile mother

Freud's case studies testify to the fact that many neurotics need a strong father figure. The well-known family romance is a kind of imaginary upgrade of the father, providing him with more authority, just as in Freud's second version of the primal horde myth. This version explains how the father is reinstalled by the son. Both the family-romance fantasy and the primal horde myth demonstrate the need for a strong, forbidding father—in order, explains Freud, to curtail the son's incestuous desire for his mother. As we saw, Freud's rewriting of the myth redefined the necessity of the father function, which has something to do with a need for protection from something arising from the woman–mother figure, although it is never very clear (in Freud, that is) what exactly this danger is about. The accent for Freud is much more on how to help the neurotic solve the problem (by installing a strong father figure) than on the underlying problem itself.

In his turn, Lacan retakes and endorses this solution, that is, the necessity for a strong and symbolically grounded father figure, although with a new attention directed toward the danger that necessitates the father's protection. Whereas Freud situates the incestuous desire in the child, Lacan sees the danger in the mother's desire for the child. For him, the paternal function (the Name-of-the-Father) is necessary to liberate the child from the mother, more particularly from the threat that supposedly comes from her desire and jouissance.

This means that Freud's formulation of the Oedipus complex, and especially the way in which he stages the father, is not so much the description of a problem as the presentation of its solution. Moreover, Freud's formulation of the Oedipus complex is an endorsement of the solution the neurotic dreams of, following a kind of fairy-tale formula: "Once upon a time, there was a real primal father who . . ." For this reason, Lacan considers the classic Oedipus complex to be Freud's own wishful dream (Lacan, 2006 [1969–70]). The neurotic subject dreams up for himself a strong father with whom he can start a reassuring fight, reassuring because it allows him to leave behind another fight and another threat. The latter are associated with the mother, albeit with the mother *as present in the imaginary of the neurotic subject.*

Freud is clinically right in his obstinate focus on the father figure, then. His mistake is that he's not aware of the fact that such a father figure is indeed the neurotic solution for an underlying neurotic problem, arising from the mother figure. Lacan brings the following correction: the Oedipus complex, in its classic version, is Freud's own dream, and the oedipal father is a construction made by the hysterical subject. This does not take away the fact that, for a long period, Lacan will make the same mistake. Like Freud, he will elevate a neurotic and hence imaginary elaboration into a theory, albeit with a shift in emphasis toward the mother.

In his theory, the mother is described as the threatening character against whom a defense is needed. In Lacan the mother is fundamentally unsatisfied, walking around "*quaerens quem devoret*" (looking for one to devour) (Lacan, 1994 [1956–57], p. 195). She is compared to a crocodile from whose jaws the only possible escape is through the phallus (Lacan, 2006 [1969–70], p. 112). As happens in Freud's theory, Lacan's reasoning also assumes mythical proportions. The mother is the *Real* (nature herself), and must be transcended by the father, that is, the *Symbolic* and culture. Only in Lacan's final theory will he distance himself from this reasoning. From then on, he will emphasize the defense against the real of the jouissance as it arises from one's own organism, and describe how both the striving for it and the defense against it get mixed up with the mother figure. At that point, he will have to redefine the castration concept as well, a step that was already more or less prepared by Freud's revision in *Moses and Monotheism* (i.e., circumcision instead of castration; pact with the father instead of punishment by the father).

Just to be clear: I do not intend to deny the existence of hyper-authoritarian fathers (primal-father style) who take pleasure in crippling their children. Devouring mothers, alas, are no mere neurotic fiction either. My criticism is aimed at a methodological error in Freud and Lacan: what they discovered in the course of their clinical practice as an anxiety and a defense against this anxiety was not analysed. Instead it was presented as a generalized theory that could be used to support their patients in their beliefs. This is exactly the opposite of what a psychoanalytic cure might offer, one creating the possibility of questioning our imaginary constructions about ourselves and our parents, constructions that we needed to cope with our drives. To instead endorse these constructions therapeutically makes such a questioning virtually impossible.

In my introduction, I mentioned the disappearance of contemporary fathers. In the light of my reasoning, it can be said that *fathers have never been sufficiently present, even when they were there in reality*. This explains the repeated and always necessary upgrading of the father figure, even if it is imaginary and even if it links him to an external guarantee. Clinical practice with neurotic patients is very instructive in this respect. Lacan describes quite aptly how the hysterical subject works very hard to put the father on a pedestal and to keep him there, mostly at the subject's own expense (Lacan, 2006 [1969–70]), followed by constant testing and endless reconfirmation of the father's elevated status. Freud did the very same thing with his theory by granting an even mythical status to the father. The need to install such a forbidding father has everything to do with an explicit need for protection against something that is situated in the woman–mother.

This brings us to Freud's second correction to his own oedipal theory. While his initial theory concerned the relation between father and son, the new part has everything to do with the daughter. This is known as the discovery of the female Oedipus complex together with the importance of the "pre"-oedipal period. Here again, we will find that the official version of this part of the theory needs to be interpreted, in order to make the shift from a hysterical version to an analytical one.

The "hystorical" version

The Freudian oedipal theory as described up to this point in many respects stands only on one leg. It focuses almost exclusively on the father–son relationship, the mother being reduced to an object. The Oedipus complex for daughters and women is totally neglected. As is well-known, until late in his career Freud disposed of the female Oedipus complex by considering it "the same as in boys, but the other way around." At the moment that he assigns the castration complex a central role, this kind of disposal becomes impossible and he has to reconsider a number of things. It is here that we'll find the importance of the "pre"-oedipal period.

Freud's autobiographical note testifies to this change. In the first version of 1925, the Oedipus complex is summarized as follows. Boys concentrate their sexual desire on their mother and, hence, develop hostile impulses against their father–rival. For the girl, an analogous situation is taken for granted, with the father as the desired object, and the mother taking the role of the rival. Ten years later, Freud adds a footnote that denounces this supposed parallel between boys and girls in matters of oedipal development (Freud, 1978 [1925d], pp. 37–39). During those ten years, he went looking for The Woman. As a result, he was confronted with the mother.

Most of the official as well as the unofficial historians agree on this part of Freud's theory, at least as far as the sequence is concerned. The founding father of psychoanalysis first of all discovered the masculine Oedipus complex. Only later did he incline his white-haired head toward the oedipal vicissitudes of women, and, as a result, produced three famous papers (Freud, 1978 [1925j, 1931b, 1933a]).[3]

This part of the Freudian theory is rather well-known, mainly because of its controversial nature (Grigg, 1999). Freud

---

[3] Strachey provides us with an enthusiastic appraisal of what he calls a first complete reassessment of Freud's views on the psychological development of women (Strachey, 1975, pp. 243–247). Jones's description contains the same content—after the Oedipus complex of the man, Freud discovered the feminine version—albeit without the enthusiasm. His controversy with Freud on this point forced him to react coldly

not only discovered the importance of the pre-oedipal mother–child relation and its effects on the oedipal development of the girl, he also formulated a number of consequences that follow on in the process of becoming a woman. It is these consequences that constitute one of the most controversial parts of psychoanalytic theory. To begin with, let us give a conventional summary of what is considered to be Freud's complete oedipal theory, including the pre-oedipal period and focusing especially on the differences between boys and girls.

For both boys and girls the mother is the first love object. For her son, she will remain the love object, both in the pre-oedipal and in the oedipal period. The intervention of the father results in a very clear-cut effect: the castration complex. Due to castration anxiety the mother will be given up as an object, and an internalization of paternal authority will take place. In this way, the male Oedipus complex ends with the formation of the superego as an effect of the fear of the castrating father (Freud, 1978 [1924d]). The prohibition against incest is installed along with the obligation for exogamy. Once having become a man, the former son gets access to sex as well, albeit with another woman. That this transition does not always run smoothly had already been described by Freud with great clinical finesse (1978 [1910h]).

(Jones, 1974, pp. 281–285). Ellenberger hastened to demonstrate that Freud's ultimate discovery of the pre-oedipal period as a determinant of the female Oedipus complex was not new at all, but was already present in Bachoven's theory on matriarchy (Ellenberger, 1970, pp. 218–223). Later, Juliet Mitchell pointed out how Freud's discovery comes down to a further development of and reaction to what he had received from women analysts (Mitchell, 1975, p. 109ff).

As a matter of fact, the discovery of the pre-oedipal period doesn't change that much in his oedipal theory concerning the man–son, with one exception. The mother is no longer reduced to a mere desired and passive object: she has become the central figure of the pre-oedipal period.

For a girl things are much more complicated. During the pre-oedipal period she has active love impulses toward the mother, just like the boy. How then does the shift to her proper love object, the father, take place? According to Freud, this is caused by her discovery of the penis and the emergence of what he calls "penis envy." The fact that she is not provided with a penis means that, besides feeling inferior and being jealous, the girl turns away in hostility from the mother to the father, hoping that she will receive what she lacks from him. The female counterpart of castration anxiety, penis envy thus becomes what *causes* the installation of the Oedipus complex, whereas for the boy it actually inaugurates the end of the oedipal period (Freud, 1978 [1925j], p. 251). For Freud, this explains why the female Oedipus complex does not have the same definite end point as the male, and why the formation of the female superego never achieves the same stringency as its male counterpart.

Freud summarized the difference between the two genders in a double displacement that is only applicable to the girl. First of all she has to change her erotogenic zone: the phallic-clitoral one has to be exchanged for the vaginal one. Secondly, the object has to be changed; the father ought to take the place of the mother (Freud, 1978 [1933a], p. 118). These two shifts can be further elucidated. The first one implies that the *active* masculine clitoris has to be exchanged for the *passive*, receiving, feminine vagina. The shift toward the father as object also carries two further implications. The penis, as the object originally desired from the father, has to be changed into the desire for a child; secondly, this child should in the end be desired from a man, her man, who has taken the place of her father. Which doesn't keep Freud from noting that a woman also looks for her mother in her later love object, just as every man does (Ibid., and 1978 [1931b], p. 230).

Considered in this way, becoming a woman is not only a very complex endeavor, but also a hopeless one. The attentive reader will have noticed that we are back to square one: we have begun with the mother and, finally, we have returned to the mother—that is, to the girl who has become a mother herself. Moreover, the whole process is directed by the man–father who is in effect producing the woman–mother. The fact that this theory has evoked a lot of negative responses, and not only from feminists, should not come as a surprise. The critique is all the stronger because clinical practice does not bring much confirmation. Indeed, the presence of penis envy is not very obvious and not every daughter turns away from her mother. Why should a girl make a shift toward the father? Freud's explanation—that the narcissistic humiliation for the girl following the discovery of her lack of a penis makes her turn away from her mother toward the father—was seriously doubted during the post-Freudian era. And even in Freud's own reasoning such a development leads to a deadlock: the girl does not become a woman; she is merely transformed into a mother herself. Thus an altogether different interpretation is possible.

An impasse is often the result of a mistaken premise. Penis envy as a motive for a change of object has to be examined a bit further. When Freud discussed penis envy as a motive for turning away from the mother, he always took care to mention a number of other motifs that are usually neglected in the post-Freudian discussions. The central one is the shift *from a passive position to an active one*; we could even say, the shift from being an object of the other toward subjectivity. Before there is any mention of penis envy or castration anxiety, the child—every child, boys as well—has already made attempts to leave the passive position in relation to the mother and to make the transition to the active one. Together with Freud, I recognize a much more basic motive in this transition: the first mother-and-child relationship, with the child as a necessarily passive object of enjoyment of the first Other because of its somatic immaturity, is dual-imaginary and as such presents an obstacle for subjectivity.[4] To put it in plain terms: there is no room for the child and its own desire, as it has only two choices. Either it follows the desire of the mother, or it refuses to do so and dies. Such a reduction to an either-or is typical for a dual-imaginary relationship as described by Lacan in his theory on the mirror stage.

The basic motive, then, is anxiety, even though this is not castration anxiety. The primal anxiety concerns this dual relation-

---

[4] The human child is born somatically premature, meaning that it is totally dependent upon its primary caretakers. It is this dependency that causes the passive position. Of course, this does not mean that an infant is not active—it is; but the focus is on "position" and on the lack of choice. This lack was aptly described by Lacan in his Seminar XI when he discussed the impossible choice at the very start of subject formation in terms of the robber's threat: "*la bourse ou la vie*" (your money or your life), (Lacan, 1994, [1964], p. 212).

ship toward the mother, our contemporary primary caretaker. The helpless infant needs the mother—hence the obvious separation anxiety. But this mother might be all too fully present, and mothering might be experienced as smothering. Freud did not pay much attention to separation anxiety, but he did recognize its less-expected counterpart: the fear of being swallowed by the mother, or being poisoned by her. Let us call this *fusion anxiety*, as the other primary anxiety, aside from separation anxiety. The concept is lacking in Freud, but the idea is there. Yet even though, in his reasoning, the first anxieties may have to do with separation and loss, he obstinately accentuates castration anxiety as the central one (Freud, 1978 [1910b], p. 8, n2).

In my understanding of Freud's concept, castration anxiety is thus a secondary and even a defensive elaboration of another, primary anxiety. The latter can take two opposite forms: the anxiety that the other will not be there when needed, or the anxiety that the other will be there far too much. Lacan's theory stresses the latter, and interprets it as the infant's anxiety about being reduced to a mere object of enjoyment by the (m)Other, as in Freud's passive position.[5] This explains the necessary

---

[5] This could very well explain Freud's penis envy too. In his reasoning, a girl has to leave her active, clitoris-based activity for a passive vaginal one. Indeed, in the Victorian era a woman was not supposed to be active. Interpreted from our reasoning, this means that she was obliged to take precisely that position that caused fear: to be a passive object of enjoyment of the other. Her reaction against such an obligation and her growing demands for an active position of her own might be the basis for Freud's idea of penis envy. In the contemporary Western world, we are witnessing exactly the opposite process; indeed, women are increasingly taking the active position, with a predictable reaction in male neurotics: flight.

function of the father in Lacanian theory: the introduction of a third party puts an end to the lack of choice that is typical for the dual-imaginary stage. The shift made possible by this introduction of the third is not so much a shift toward the father away from the mother as it is a shift from duality toward triangularity. From that point onward, subjectivity and choice become possible.

The analytical version

The idea that the Oedipus complex is preceded by a "pre-oedipal" period delineates a respective focus on the subject's father or mother. The theater of the Oedipus complex, in its totality, casts both figures. It starts with the mother as the central character: she is the first love object for every child, independently of its gender. This first relationship has a very characteristic role distribution. On the one hand, there is the mother as the incarnation of active power, either refusing or giving—or, worse, absent. At the other side, we find the infant in the passive, receiving position where choice is limited to acceptance or refusal. The so-called feelings of omnipotence of the adult neurotic do not go back to a supposed infantile omnipotence, but to an infantile identification with *the mother's* omnipotence. Indeed: "*Ce que la femme veut, Dieu le veut*" (What woman wants, God wants as well) should read: "*Ce que la maman veut, Dieu le veut*" (What mother wants, God wants as well)—as little Hans already knew. To state it more clearly: the adult neurotic's feelings of omnipotence go back to an infantile identification with a phallic mother (Lacan, 1994 [1956–57]). Meaning: the mother without a lack, as she is perceived by the child. Paranoia shows us the pathological forms this relationship can take, more particularly in the fear of being killed by the mother, of being devoured, of being poisoned (Freud, 1978 [1931b], pp. 226, 237).

Freud remarks that passivity always entails a particular reaction, namely an active repetition of the things one had to undergo passively (Freud, 1978 [1931b], p. 235). The pre-oedipal mother–child relationship is no exception to this rule. The child wants to perform actively what it had to endure passively from the mother. A first transition concerns the step from being suckled to active sucking, which can even take an oral-sadistic dimension. In case of pathology, the duality in this is unmistakable; the aggressive oral-sadistic impulses toward the mother find their counterpart in the fear of being killed by her.

The example of orality is not a coincidence. Indeed, the two opposing poles—activity versus passivity—have to do with a dimension of *enjoyment* in the mother-and-child relationship. The attempts of the child (and not only those of the girl) to make the transition from the passive pole to the active one must be understood as a running away from the position of being a passive object of enjoyment (of the mother) toward an active control of pleasure. In his very early theories, Freud had put forward the ideas of seduction by the father and infantile sexual trauma as the basis for neurosis. The omnipresence of neurosis obliged him to take his distance from this idea, although he never really abandoned it (Freud, letter to Fliess, September 21, 1897 [1978 (1892–99)]). Thirty years later, he reformulated these ideas. The original seduction is nothing but the nursing situation. The mother "seduces" the child to a certain form of enjoyment. It is only later on, in the final oedipal stage, that this position of seductor will be shifted to the father in the child's imagination.

At last Freud had discovered a real basis for the supposed omnipresence of traumatic seduction: every nursing situation is potentially seductive and enjoyable. The traumatic and hence frightening aspect in the very same situation has to do with the fact that it reduces the subject to the position of being the passive object of the enjoyment of the other. The primary version of such a relationship is the early oedipal bond between mother and child. The exit from this duality is made possible by a third figure, the father, in combination with a shift from passive to active position.

Within the early Lacanian framework the parallel line of reasoning runs as follows: the child is in origin a passive object of the mother's enjoyment within a dual relationship. This jouissance cannot be signified as it is situated outside the phallic order of signifiers. Normally, the intervention of the father introduces the Symbolic order via which signification and regulation are introduced. Notice again that in this reasoning, both in Freud and in Lacan, the danger is situated in the mother and the salvation in the father. The difference between them resides in the fact that, for Lacan, the accent is on the *symbolic* function of the father—not on the father himself, let alone on a primal father. As we will see later, this symbolic function installs an opening, a lack, and hence the very possibility of choice.

Jouissance and passivity

Generally, it is said that Freud first discovered the Oedipus complex in relation to the male and that *Totem and Taboo* was an anthropological application of this discovery, an excursion of applied psychoanalysis into anthropology. It was only later on that Freud was supposed to have concentrated on the feminine Oedipus complex, resulting in the discovery of the importance of the pre-oedipal period in the process of becoming a woman.

We've seen, though, that Freud's first conceptualization of the oedipal period is not the masculine version, but rather the *hysterical* version, in which Freud followed in the footsteps of the hysteric to create a certain solution for an underlying problem, one the full extent of which Freud did not entirely understand at that time. The solution was to introduce an almighty father figure, a change that did not take place without difficulties; to these, *Totem and Taboo* was Freud's answer. Through this self-constructed myth Freud provided a guarantee for the existence of the particular father figure needed by the neurotic to solve this very problem.

However, the nature of the problem itself was not very clear in the first oedipal theory. Prohibition of incest in relation to the mother was not accounted for by the myth of the primal horde. Conversely, there emerged another prohibition, the one against enjoying all women as the primal father did. Freud's discovery of the pre-oedipal period and the mother–child relationship that typifies it allows us to understand this prohibition as a protection. Freud's second version of the primal horde myth lets it be understood that the first mother-and-child relationship contains a risk—even a threat—emanating from the woman–mother against which the paternal authority has to provide protection. At least, that is the way this anxiety is presented, with the woman–mother in the bad role of the dangerous character. During the longer part of his career, Lacan will endorse this idea and even give it a further elaboration in which the maternal danger similarly takes on mythical proportions.

To restate this, Freud's oedipal theory did not begin with the initial discovery of the masculine Oedipus complex followed by the discovery of the feminine version. That supposedly masculine version is nothing but a defensive setup via the creation of an imagined authoritarian oedipal father, one for which Freud provided historical roots. Only afterward did he discover what this defense was directed against. And this goes for both genders. The true starting point is the early oedipal relationship between the first Other and the infant, characterized by an enjoyment beyond the signifier that is described by Freud as passivity. This form of jouissance contains a threat, and it is precisely to protect against this threat that the authoritarian father is constructed. In order to be able to understand this, we must turn to a complex chapter in Lacan's theory.

jouissance

Introduction

Up to a point, Lacan confirms and amplifies or expands on Freud's oedipal theory. With his formula of the paternal metaphor he describes in structural terms the mechanism by which a child becomes disentangled from his mother via the intervention, not of the father himself, but of what he calls "the Name-of-the-Father" (Lacan, 1977 [1955–56], p. 200; 1994 [1956–57], p. 379). The religious connotations of this concept, underlined by the use of capitals, are quite clear and may elicit an almost automatic aversion. Lacan's anti-maternal remarks combined with this implicit deification of the patriarchal are indeed quite reminiscent of Catholic doctrine (Tort, 2000). If we manage to get past this aversion, we can see that this formula presents two main differences from Freud's theory.

We've already discussed the first: in Lacan, the prohibition arising from the father is not directed toward the child, but toward the mother. It is her desire, even her jouissance, that is threatening. As we saw, this idea is implicit in Freud's second version of his myth. Secondly, with the Name-of-the-Father Lacan introduces a distinction between the figure and the function of the father. Any particular father is only able to take up a certain function of authority because his position is guaranteed by the Symbolic order and its inherent laws, and the conventions regulating human interactions. For Lacan, the oedipal period is nothing less than the transition from nature to culture, with a nod to Lévi-Strauss (1969 [1949]). As in Freud, this reasoning depends on a reciprocal guarantee.[1] The Symbolic order guarantees both the Name-of-the-Father and the law (incest prohibition and obligation for exogamy). At the same time, it is the Name-of-the-Father that founds the Symbolic order and its inherent laws. The father then, as a concrete figure, receives his authority from the fact that he acts as a representative of that guarantee, and that is his function.

---

[1] Concisely formulated as follows: "It is in the *name of the father* that we must recognize the basis of the symbolic function which, since the dawn of historical time, has identified his person with the figure of the law" (Lacan, 2006 [1966], p. 230).

In practice, the coming and going of the mother is not predictable for the infant, meaning that her desire is not predictable and hence threatening. It is threatening for the infant to be dependent on someone who may or may not be there for unknown reasons. The moment that it becomes clear that the mother has another interest beyond the child, that is, that her coming and going is also determined by her desire for the father, the infant's sense of being engulfed by the mother's desire abates as the child is able to signify the mother's desire in symbolic, phallic terms. This means that she also is subjected to regulation, namely to society's laws and structures, as signified via the Name-of-the-Father (Lacan, 2006 [1966], p. 464ff). As his theory continues to evolve, this difference between figure (the father) and function (Name-of-the-Father, signifier for the Law) remains, with the figure becoming less and less important.

Despite these dissimilarities Lacan's theory up to this point is not fundamentally different from Freud's. But quite soon after introducing the paternal metaphor Lacan presents in 1960[2] the idea of a structurally determined lack in the Symbolic order and hence in the Other (Lacan, 2006 [1966], pp. 793ff).[3] This marks

---

[2] Lacan's work—just like Freud's for that matter—is not a logical-temporal corpus in which new insights come on top of older ones. If this were the case, we could truly speak in terms of Lacan's "first" theory, his "second," and so on. As a matter of fact, his conceptualization is much more complex, with ideas of the "last" Lacan already present in early papers, and vice versa. When I talk about his "last theory," I am presenting my interpretation of what I consider to be the strong accents in his final productions.

[3] The necessity for a structurally determined opening or lack in a symbolic system in order to make the functioning of this system possible can be logically demonstrated by Gödel's theorem. A less complicated way to demonstrate the same necessity can be achieved through a toy, a so-called gliding-puzzle. If one wants to put

a radical departure from his (and Freud's) previous reasoning, and introduces something so radically new that it can barely be expressed in Freudian terms. The Name-of-the-Father is no longer the guarantee of the Other, that is, of the Symbolic order, and vice versa. On the contrary: there is no Other of the Other ("*il n'y a pas d'Autre de l'Autre*"). Previously, the Name-of-the-Father had guaranteed the (function of the) father, just as Freud's primal father grounded every father. Now, what the Name-of-the-Father guarantees is the *lack* in the Other, or the symbolic castration of the subject.[4] And it is via this symbolic castration that the subject may leave an all-embracing determinism and come to his or her own choices, limited as they may be.

The repercussions of this change reverberate through all of Lacan's subsequent work, right to the very end, like a wave that keeps rolling indefinitely, and indeed the theory's most es-

---

the pieces in the correct order, one has to shift them around. In order to be able to shift them, you need an opening, one space lacking an element. Otherwise everything is literally and figuratively stuck. Both the lack and the possibility of shifting (see metonymy) are essential characteristics of every symbolic system.

[4] In matters of transference this new theory has important implications that demonstrate its radical reversal when compared to Freud. Based upon his theory and probably his personality as well, Freud used to take the guaranteeing paternal position vis-à-vis his patients. Based upon Lacanian reasoning, the analyst—insofar as she or he wants to guarantee something—will take the opposite stance, that is, the analyst will guarantee that there is no final closure, that there is a lack and an opening in matters of desire and enjoyment. This is close to what Benjamin describes as the condition for the installation of the "third" during an analysis, or the recognition by the analyst of his or her own lack (Benjamin, 2004, p. 32). The irony of the history is that in this respect many post-Lacanians are more Freudian than Lacanian in their presentation of authoritarian arguments: something is guaranteed to be true because it is in Lacan . . . A number of post-Lacanians are fighting each other, using quotations of the master (necessarily always a selective practice) as their sole arguments. The step toward empirical clinical research is rather rare, and such discussions remind me of the long-gone times of scholastics.

sential message is that no theory will ever be complete.[5] The closed system set up by the circular reasoning that we found before in both Freud and Lacan (the father is guaranteed by the primal father and/or the Name-of-the-Father, and vice versa) is with one stroke superseded. At the same time, a new problem emerges. What is the binding or uniting element in a symbolic order that is based on a structural lack? This problem may seem to be an academic one, but it is not. Ultimately, the question concerns the binding element in one's identity. Up until now, Lacan had always stressed the fundamental alienation and splitting in subjectivity, leaving aside the feeling of unity. The latter was supposed to be an effect of the Name-of-the-Father. When he leaves this theory, he has to produce another explanation for the subjective feeling of unity in one's identity. Lacan continues restlessly to reformulate and rephrase these terms—from the plural in the "Names-of-the-Father" to the supposedly founding and quite axiomatic "there is oneness" (*Il y a de l'Un*), (Lacan, 1999 [1972–73], pp. 141–143)—but his continual questioning does not serve to clarify matters, and a final

[5] In 1964, Lacan wanted to give a seminar on "the names-of-the-father," a concept that, compared to his previous theory, endorses this shift by putting the previous "Name-of-the-Father" in the plural. At that moment, the International Psychoanalytic Association decided that his teaching would no longer be recognized as part of psychoanalytic training (in France). Lacan experienced this as banishment and, as a result, never gave this seminar (notice: because of a "paternal" no). The irony of the case is that the continuing post-Lacanian movement has invested this seminar with a meaning that is perfectly coherent with its lacking content, albeit either in a symbolic or in an imaginary way. For some of them it illustrates the structurally grounded lack: the basis of the Symbolic order can never be spoken. For others, the lack keeps its imaginary function of a guarantee: the master could have said it but chose not to.

answer is lacking. Ironically, this is quite coherent with the essence of this new theory.

Looking back toward Lacan's starting point, we can see that there is an increasing demythologization of the father and even of the function of the father as we go forward. Even in Lacan, then, we find a progressive weakening of the importance of the father, just as in Anglo-Saxon psychoanalysis. This does not take away the fact that a major part of Lacan's theory lends itself to a classic interpretation based upon a patriarchal point of view. In the post-Lacanian interpretation, this is usually understood as follows: the woman–mother is the dangerous character whose enjoyment has to be restrained (Lacan, 1991 [1969–70], p. 129). Thereby, the (Name of the) father functions as the safeguarding figure based on his phallic position, from which he can free the child from the threatening maternal desire. Such a reading—that soon enough turns into mother-blaming and ends with a plea for strong fathers—is not at all rare in Lacanian theory. Lacan may be remembered primarily as the preeminent patriarchal phallocrat for whom Symbolic order and masculine principle were synonymous in a so-called "logo-phallo-centrism." From my point of view, it is much more interesting to ask about the reasons for this kind of construction. It becomes even more interesting when we observe that Lacan himself presents us with arguments for answering this question.

Moreover, this criticism is only correct to a certain extent. From 1969 onward, Lacan's theory went in another direction, demanding a different discussion. The central concept becomes jouissance—enjoyment—albeit with a new meaning. Previously he'd described jouissance as the not-symbolized, real part of the drive of the (m)Other, threatening the subject. In that part of the theory, the dangerous "jouissance of the Other" and "other jouissance" blended together: the jouissance of the Other is the mother's jouissance at the expense of her offspring; feminine jouissance is really an "other" jouissance, compared to the phallic one.[6] The combined woman–mother is like the praying mantis that devours her male after the copulation (Lacan, 2003 [1962–63]). In Seminar XVII with its telling title, *The Other Side of Psycho-Analysis*, Lacan argues that both the mother and the father are little more than pawns in a social shadow-play, a kind of chess game that is the Oedipus complex. As I will explain, the result is that an original impossibility of jouissance will become hidden behind a prohibition, thus creating an illusion for the subject that she or he might transcend this prohibition (ibid., pp. 74, 79).

Jouissance?

What exactly, then, does the concept *jouissance* denote? Lacan will never define it very clearly, providing us with only vague indications. This imprecision is deliberate. For Lacan, enjoyment is by definition indefinable; it is that which escapes symbolization (Lacan, 2006 [1969–70], pp. 176–177). Although we find

---

[6] Phallic jouissance is Freud's pleasure, meaning abreaction and reduction of tension, with the orgasm as the most prominent example. This phallic jouissance—orgasm—goes both for male and female. But even Freud had to recognize that there is another pleasure at work, beyond his phallic pleasure principle, aiming at the opposite goal, namely the building up of tensions. In my reading, this is what Lacan understands by the "other" jouissance.

no parallel concept in Freud, it is in his writing about the pleasure principle that Lacan found the suggestion of the idea of jouissance (Freud, 1978 [1920g]). There must be something "beyond" (*jenseits*) the pleasure principle, Freud concludes, even working *against* it and serving, furthermore, as the cause of a strange repetition—strange, because what is repeated is not necessarily what could be called pleasure. In fact, jouissance might be the opposite of pleasure: "*Unlust*," or "*déplaisir*" (Lacan, 2007 [1969–70], p. 77).[7]

This leads to an unexpected conclusion, although *The Psychopathology of Everyday Life* provides us with ample support for it: mankind takes a very ambivalent stance toward enjoyment. On the one hand the attempt to repeat it is installed in an almost automatic way. On the other, it seems as if there is an instinctual brake being applied against the attempt to regain any experience of jouissance. This was probably Freud's first psychoanalytical discovery and forms the very basis of his theory: in every subject there is an internal division at work in combination with a defense directed against one's own desire and satisfaction. Initially, he found an explanation for this *Abwehr* and internal splitting in the frustrating effects of Victorian society, but soon it became clear to him that this explanation was not going far enough (Freud, 1978 [1896], p. 222).

We meet here with a surprising question, though the surprise has to do with our naive postmodern expectation. Why

[7] In this respect, translating *jouissance* in terms of pleasure causes problems. We choose to keep it in its original form, jouissance. Sometimes we will use "enjoyment," purely for reasons of style.

would someone be afraid of his or her own enjoyment? Why don't we go all the way all the time, especially in our contemporary permissive society? The problem of pleasure, says Freud, is one of the most difficult issues to understand in human psychology. In his original conception, pleasure came down to reduction of tension via discharge, with the (phallic) orgasm as the most prominent example. The pleasure principle aims to install a level of tension that is as low as possible and preferably constant. Later on, Freud had to discover that there is a beyond to his beloved pleasure principle, in which another form of enjoyment is at work, albeit one that is the exact opposite of the so-called normal pleasure. Indeed, it has everything to do with a rise in tension, something that in his first understanding was considered to be only painful. In his final theory, Freud tries to understand these two opposite forms of pleasure by linking them to two basic drives that would govern everything and do so independently of the whims and desires of any actual individual. This independence can even go so far that an individual might do things that she or he doesn't want to do, hence the literal idea of being driven by one's drive and the irresistible urge. Being overwhelmed by it is an ever-existing and threatening possibility.

Moreover, these two drives aim at exactly opposite goals, which are fusion for the one that Freud will call Eros, and separation for the other that he will denominate rather unfortunately as Thanatos, each with its own form of pleasure. From this point forward, we can suggest an answer to our question why we don't go "all the way." We can't, first of all because there are two conflicting ways, and secondly, because each way has a final price that the subject cannot afford. The Thanatos drive is the easiest to understand. It strives for discharge and zero tension—with death as the final stage and orgasm as a lively stepping-stone toward it. For Freud, the aim of Thanatos is separation and the splitting of larger unities into ever-smaller fragments. On the level of the subject this means separation from the other and an intensified individuality—I am here, *I* do exist as a separate human being. The aim of Eros is exactly the opposite: fusion and uniting different elements into one bigger whole in which the individual elements tend to lose their individuality. Life is a conglomerate of ever-increasing tension that is pure enjoyment, although not for the individual—the latter disappears into it and is quite afraid of this disappearance, a barrier that is translated rather meekly by contemporary psychology as the "fear of losing control." And it is not only control that is lost; even the controller him- or herself disappears during the process.

Going solely for the Thanatos drive leaves us alone and finally dead. Going exclusively for the Eros drive makes us disappear as well, this time into a larger unity. Both of them have their own enjoyment, and each human being has to map his or her own road between the two of them. Freud remarks that in normal circumstances both drives are mixed—the *Triebmischung*—in the ever-changing cocktail of each individual life.

Lacan continues this Freudian reasoning. Jouissance and death are quite close; the road to jouissance is the road to death as well, hence the ambivalent stance of the subject toward jouissance (Lacan, 2006 [1969–70], p. 18). Jouissance as such is impossible for the living subject, as it implies its own death. The only possibility left is to take a roundabout route, repeating it in order to postpone as long as possible one's arrival at the destination.

For Lacan, this has to do with a fundamental characteristic of the living. In his reasoning, the instinctual brake on jouissance is in place well before there is such a thing as a divided subject or even a human identity. Before the actual onset of subject formation, the opposition against jouissance is already at work via the Other, that is, in that which will determine the formation of the subject. In other words, both jouissance and the opposition to it are an essential part of the process that determines the formation of the subject. It appears in a certain role distribution. The division of roles comes down to the mother getting the part of the jouissance, the father the part of the brake operator. The original ambivalence toward jouissance becomes incarnate in concrete characters. For Lacan, this incarnation is precisely the Oedipus complex. Its result is called castration, which applies not only to mother and child but to the father as well. That the concepts of fatherhood, motherhood, and castration take on a new meaning here—when compared to previous theories—is an understatement.

But then, where does this jouissance come from? From the Other, says Lacan. The "Other" now has a different meaning.[8] The trouble is that Lacan continues to use his standard expression—"the jouissance of the Other"—although its meaning has changed. Here, it indicates *one's own body* as the most fundamental Other, in fact our real organism as the most intimate stranger. The importance of this shift in Lacan's thinking becomes

[8] This answer sounds easy, but it hides a complex evolution that I will not address here. For a detailed study of Lacan's theory in this respect, see Verhaeghe, 2001, pp. 65–132, and 2006.

clearer when we remember that, previously, the Other in the very same expression ("the jouissance of the Other") referred to the woman–mother.

So, jouissance arises from one's own body, more particularly from its border zones (mouth, anus, genitals, eyes, ears, skin; Lacan had discussed this already in his Seminar XI). Anxiety concerning jouissance then is basically anxiety about being overwhelmed by one's own drive and enjoyment. The fact that a defense against it shifts to a defense against the (m)Other has everything to do with the typical developmental process within a given social structure.

Our body is the Other that enjoys, if possible together with us, if need be without us. To make things even more complicated, the original meaning of the "Other" is still present alongside the new meaning, although a little changed. That there is some contamination between the two meanings is no coincidence. On one hand we have the Other as the body from which the jouissance arises; on the other there is the Other as the (m)Other who provides access to this jouissance via signifiers. Indeed, in Lacan's new theory the subject acquires access to the enjoyment of its own body *only via the signifiers coming from the Other* (called "markings"). This explains why the (m)Other becomes "the seat of enjoyment" against whom defense is necessary.

Role of the mother: Seat of a forbidden enjoyment

Jouissance comes from the body, the body as a substance that enjoys. Since Lacan based his ideas regarding pleasure on Freud's, we can assume that this has to do with different levels of tension and with a classic opposition between charging and discharging. Jouissance takes place on the body, through invasions ("*éruptions de jouissance*").[9] These invasions get marked, that is, they are inscribed on the body through the intervention (performative and verbal) of the Other (Lacan, 2006 [1969–70], pp. 49–50). If one wants to travel the road to jouissance again, one is inevitably obliged to follow the signs that have previously been erected along this road by the Other who marked them (ibid., p. 78). In almost every case this Other is the mother, more particularly the caretaking and name-giving mother. Lacan states that jouissance can only ever be experienced by the subject on two conditions: the jouissance has to be inscribed, and its repetition has to center on these inscriptions. The oyster "knows" no enjoyment because it lacks a signifier. At most, it can only "be" enjoyment, a "being of enjoyment" (ibid., p. 177). The human subject is the exception because she or he knows jouissance via the markings based upon the signifiers coming from the Other. Without these, the subject, like the oyster, wouldn't "know" the jouissance. In

---

[9] This is an important change in Lacan's theory. Previously, in his Seminar VII on ethics (Lacan, 1992 [1959–60]), jouissance was conceived of as belonging exclusively to the Real and was therefore diametrically opposed to the Symbolic. In such a perspective, enjoyment could be reached only through *transgression* of the law. In Seminar XVII, *The Other Side of Psycho-Analysis*, in contrast, jouissance is of the order of an *invasion* (Lacan, 2006 [1969–70], pp. 19–20). This has everything to do with his new understanding of the relationship between the real part in the jouissance and the Symbolic. Lacan puts forward an original relationship between jouissance and the signifier. He even goes so far as to consider that the very origin of the signifier has to be looked for precisely in the marking processes of the enjoyment by the Other. In reverse perspective, the subject has to use the signifier to rediscover the jouissance—yet this necessarily results in a failure and in getting stuck on the road toward it. Lacan will argue that this failure is necessary. It is the road itself that is the aim of the living.

this way, Lacan brings together the "Other of the body" (jouissance) and "the Other of the signifier" (inscriptions).

The seed of this reasoning can be found in Freud when he indicated how every mother "seduces" her child while caring for it. Indeed, the nursing activities are always focusing on the border areas of the body, the same areas where enjoyment is situated (mouth, anus, genitals, skin, eye, ear). In Seminar XX (Lacan, 1999 [1972–73], p. 23), Lacan describes the real body as an "enjoying substance" whereby the initial experiences of jouissance (or invasions) simultaneously imply their inscription on the body (ibid., p. 89). This is their "use value," but in itself this does not suffice if we are talking about jouissance in terms of the subject. No doubt the oyster will also have a "use value." The necessary supplement is the mother's intervention that marks the invasions of jouissance in the course of her interaction with her child. Through these interventions, the original use value is entered into a dialectical exchange between subject and Other, and the experiences of jouissance acquire an "exchange value." In concrete terms this means that for the subject *everything in matters of jouissance has to pass through the Other.* Lacan rediscovers his own theory of the mirror stage here, albeit with a different focus. The mother is a particular source of identity, as she provides the marking signifiers via which the subject obtains access to jouissance. As a result, the mother becomes the source of jouissance as well.

It is not that difficult to see the link with contemporary infant mentalization and attachment theory here, where it is also said that the infant learns to know its bodily experiences via the other's mirroring (Fonagy et al., 2002). The responses they refer to somewhat mildly in terms of "affect" and "arousal" are what Lacan terms the "invasions" of jouissance. The subject has to experience his or her own jouissance—the very jouissance arising from one's own body—as coming from the Other.[10] As a consequence, it is also with and via the Other that a subject must rediscover the road toward this jouissance. Here, the Other has several meanings: it stands for one's own body and also for the other of flesh and blood, as well as for the signifier.

It is not by accident that Lacan refers in this context to Freud's idea of the lost object, the mythical primordial satisfaction that can never be found again (Lacan, 2006 [1969–70], p. 50), and the acts of repetition that ensue after its loss. Defined in this way, the Other receives a positive meaning. More often than not, this more positive side is overlooked and the focus is on the dangerous, even deadly aspect in jouissance and on the necessary defense against it. By association, the Other receives this negative meaning as well. Indeed, if the subject needs a defense against jouissance, she or he will very rapidly turn that defense into one against the Other. This confusion is almost inevitable since the confusion between jouissance and (m)Other is installed in the subject from the very beginning.

The repercussions of this confusion go very far. This explains why women have been assumed to be the seat of a threatening passion, even a lasciviousness, that has to be damped down because otherwise it might destroy both themselves and men. This

---

[10] It is in Seminar XX (Lacan, 1999 [1972–73]) that the "jouissance of the Other" takes on an ambiguous expression, as "the Other" becomes both the body and the Other who marks the jouissance on that body, namely the (m)Other.

is the underlying reasoning that explains Freud's second version of his primal myth and—by and large—his oedipal theory. The child is in need of a strong father who will protect him by prohibiting access to the mother and, by extension, to the dangerous jouissance that is associated with her. This also explains Lacan's first oedipal theory: it is the mother who might enjoy her child in an almost deadly way and it is only via the intervention of the father that the subject is saved from her possibly lethal enjoyment. And it is the same reasoning that we find in an increasing way in the three religions of the book, beginning with Eve as the source of all evil, passing through the Catholic anxiety about and hate of sex and women, and ending with the Muslim obligation for the wearing of chadors and the like. Women have to be kept at bay because they might seduce men and cause their fall. This should read: our own jouissance, arising from our own body, is not only enjoyable but obviously also something threatening that we need to control; it follows that the easiest way to control it is by assigning it to the other and—if need be—by destroying this other.[11]

Indeed, this developmentally based link between jouissance and the other opens the way for the subject to externalize a conflict concerning jouissance that might otherwise remain internal. The subject's divided stance is based upon an instinctual knowledge that jouissance leads to death and hence has to

---

[11] In our contemporary Western society, where the primary caretaker might be the father and where gender equality has been more or less installed, we can increasingly see the same reaction from women vis-à-vis men, that is, women accusing men for flaunting their erotic appeal while at the same time ignoring their own drive and enjoyment.

be slowed down, if not avoided altogether. As Freud indicated repeatedly, one can escape an internal threat only by projecting it into the external world. The trouble is that in matters of jouissance, this external world is almost synonymous with woman . . .

Jouissance is marked by the signifiers of the Other, through which the subject acquires knowledge about its own jouissance. If for one reason or another some bodily area and/or activity is marked by the mother more than other areas or activities, one can be sure that it will take a prominent role in adult life. During this process, the original use value is turned into an exchange value and the Other becomes the entrance gate to jouissance via her markings. Thereby, our originally divided stance toward our own enjoyment—founded on an instinctual knowledge that the road to enjoyment leads to death—becomes, from the point of the introduction of the Other's markings onward, externalized and redistributed via those characters that incarnate the Other. In order to repeat jouissance, one has to ask the first Other—the entry lies with her. Yet at the very same time this Other also receives a stamp saying "forbidden," in order to install the necessary brake. Hence, the possibility of and the prohibition on jouissance are installed in one and the same figure: the woman–mother. The task of translating the impossibility of jouissance into a prohibition is ascribed to yet another figure: the father.

Lacan calls this a "cunning" transition that, almost unnoticed, replaces the intrinsic impossibility of jouissance with a prohibition of enjoyment. It is only through our social structures that this prohibition can be implemented; ever since Freud, the result has been known as the Oedipus complex. For Lacan, this amounts to a "social complicity" by which mankind deceives itself. Indeed, reframing impossibility in terms of prohibition leaves us with the illusion that we might surpass this prohibition and attain a supreme form of enjoyment.[12] Hence the strange association between desire and prohibition: whatever might be prohibited is immediately imbued and suffused with a surplus of imagined enjoyment, and vice versa. Again, this is nothing but the Oedipus complex, in whatever form it may appear to take among different cultures.

Like it or not, woman unavoidably takes on a central role in this complex. As a mother, she produces and hence dominates the inscriptions of jouissance; any attempt to repeat jouissance must be addressed to her.[13] The child becomes the demanding party and inhabits a position of dependence with respect to her. Whereas the original (im)possibility of jouissance was previously located in the living body as a "being of enjoyment," the possibility of jouissance and the simultaneous need for its failure are now projected onto the mother. By means of social complicity the child is fixated onto the mother, as she becomes the elected

---

[12] Its most subtle formulation was already presented in Seminar VII (Lacan, 1992 [1959–60]) as courtly love. In this form of relationship, the love object is described as forbidden and unreachable by the lover himself. This permits the lover to keep up appearances ("I decide") and to avoid acknowledging the intrinsic impossibility.

[13] In the full version, the infant first of all has to produce an appeal to the mother, based on a combination of drive arousal and its helplessness. The mother's answer (see the mirror stage) operates in a regulating, marking, and satisfying way. Once the child wants to find the same (regulation of the) jouissance again, it has to address a demand to the mother, and consequently it has to identify itself with the answer of the mother and hence with the marking points that she has already produced. Notice that the underlying reasoning here is quite close to certain ideas of Chodorow (1999).

seat of both an absolute enjoyment and its prohibition (Lacan, 2006 [1969–70], p. 79).

The question then is, What remains of the original jouissance? Again, Lacan answers with an equivocal expression: "*le plus-de-jouir.*" In French, this can be understood both as "not enjoying any more" and as "more of the enjoyment." The jouissance that remains for the subject after its defensive elaboration is less than and different from the original form and will never be fully satisfactory.

It is the mother as Other who leads her little one toward the *plus-de-jouir*, that is, the roads toward a (limited) enjoyment are opened for the child on condition that it renounce a supposedly original and total jouissance that from now on will be imagined to be situated in the mother (Lacan, 2006 [1969–70], p. 78). This limited enjoyment will never be experienced as enough; hence the fundamental lack of satisfaction and the perpetual need for an *encore*.

Comparing these ideas to Lacan's earlier understanding of the mother-woman role brings out some glaring differences. Before, the woman–mother, the Real, drive, and jouissance denominated a more or less common anxiety-provoking threat. Protection against it was expected in one way or another from the man–father, the Symbolic, and the phallic signifier; again, these terms denominated a more or less common institution. In Lacan's later theory, the mother is reduced to someone who gets a role assignment without having asked for it and with hardly a possibility for refusal. And she has to pay a price for it as well. She may become a desired object, but at the very same time she becomes above all a forbidden object, an object that is purported to be quite dangerous should one be able to reach her beyond this prohibition. *La femme fatale* appears as a product of this oedipal theater.[14]

How does the role of the father figure in all of this? As we saw, Freud's theory is contradictory in this respect. Analysis of his self-produced myth yielded surprising results. As Lacan observes, in Freud's model the result of the primal murder is exactly the opposite of its aim (Lacan, 2006 [1969–70], pp. 118–120). Indeed, instead of opening the gateway toward sexually enjoying the women, the original jouissance becomes definitively unreachable. Lacan concludes (against Freud) that the murder of the primal father is what installs the prohibition of jouissance. Important as this correction may be, it does not make the myth or the idea of a primal father more acceptable. Redefining the father role is therefore one of the major endeavors of his Seminar XVII and it is no coincidence that it is entitled *The Other Side of Psycho-Analysis* (*L'Envers de la psychanalyse*, 1991 [1969–70]).

Role of the father: The structural operator of the prohibition

By means of the social apparatus, then, the impossibility of jouissance is translated into a prohibition, whereby the two

---

[14] The irony of subject formation or identity acquisition is that a number of women will identify themselves with this position of femme fatale, thereby confirming the male's anxious desire. Indeed, the main process in subject formation is the identification with the signifiers presented by the Other, be it a particular person or the Other of the advertisement and fashion business . . . Lacan referred to this as alienation, which is not a bad idea at all. Every femme fatale feels alienated in the role she is playing for the benefit of herself and the Other.

genders get different role assignments. Absolute jouissance is impossible and this has nothing to do with a mother who does or doesn't want to respond to her child, nor with an almighty father who prohibits his children from enjoying their mother. Both of them are determined by an impossibility that exists a priori and especially by the way in which this impossibility is molded by the social apparatus and the distribution of roles. Of course, it is quite possible for an actual mother and father to link their private pathology to these roles, just as it is possible that a private pathology will be determined to a certain extent by the distribution of roles. In its turn, this will have serious effects on the couple's offspring, as illustrated by clinical practice. In the context of this essay, I want to concentrate on the structural effects and on the theory.

Lacan's reworking of the role of the father in Seminar XVII distances itself from any psychologizing, moralizing interpretations, even the ones he himself has made about crocodile mothers and liberating fathers. Freud's idea of an almighty father, enjoying all women, is now described as an illusion; the father is scarcely capable of satisfying one woman (Lacan, 2006 [1969–70], pp. 100, 124). Lacan's thesis is that man and woman, father and mother, are inevitably pushed into certain positions on the basis of a preexisting fact: the impossibility of jouissance. The role assigned to the father in and via the social game is indeed one of prohibiting. Beyond this role assignment, Lacan rethinks the function of the father in a structural way that enables him to put a different theory of castration to the fore. Instead of Freud's castrating primal father, he will present us with the castrated and even humiliated father. The distance from Freud's ideas is of such magnitude that a new term is required, hence *symbolic* castration. This father has one task, to hand on to his child a certain function, the master signifier or the S_1, without which identity formation would not be possible. Every one of us needs such a master signifier without lack or division with which we can pretend to coincide—in short, a "That's me" signifier.[15] It is only afterward that we can permit ourselves the luxury of doubt.

For Freud, the accent is on the negative part, that is, castration anxiety in the boy and penis envy in the girl. Because of these, the neurotic subject will never be able to reach full satisfaction, although it seems as if this satisfaction is waiting just around the corner, so to speak. This illusion was very much cherished by the post–May '68 society (ironically, it was in 1968 that Lacan showed the fallacy of this construct). Our contemporary postmodern capitalist society has even reinforced it: jouissance can be bought, it lies waiting just one mouse click away.

Going against Freud's theory, Lacan defines castration as a structural consequence of human development. Here one must understand that from the moment we speak we lose our direct contact with the Real, precisely because we speak. In particular, we lose our direct contact with the real of our own body. This is symbolic castration, and it reinforces the original impossibility of jouissance because the subject must proceed by way of the signi-

[15] For Lacan our original identity is first of all not original at all, as it comes from the Other's mirroring; secondly, our identity is a divided one, because it is based on signifiers (again: coming from the Other as presented by different others) that convey conflicting desires. A master signifier is the one and only exception, as it is the signifier that is identical to itself, without a lack or division. Our name is the most prominent example of it.

fier if she or he wants to attain the jouissance of the body. Thus, the impossibility of jouissance receives a concrete form for the speaking subject. On the one hand the path to jouissance is paved with signifiers because of the markings coming from the Other. On the other, the very use of these signifiers now has a consequence: the jouissance will never be fully reached. This has to do with the gap between the Symbolic and the Real: it is not possible for the signifier to hold the real of the jouissance completely.[16]

In social terms the implementation of this structural given links woman and jouissance, father and prohibition, both of these combined with a typical fantasy—the lethal jouissance of the femme fatale, the wrath of the father–castrator. Jouissance is assigned to woman because it is the (m)Other who has marked the invasions of jouissance on the body of the child. The child's "own" jouissance comes from the Other.[17] The need to keep jouissance at bay and to create a halt on the road to jouissance next takes the form of defining both the mother and her jouissance as prohib-

---

[16] In his Seminar XX (Lacan, 1999 [1972–73]), Lacan introduces in this respect the notion of the "not-whole" (*le pas-tout*), which is just another way of saying that the Symbolic order is never complete. It is structurally impossible for the Symbolic order to completely match the Real: there will always be a remainder. The gap between the Symbolic and the Real is the very same as that between body and soul, psyche and soma.

[17] Notice that "the Other" again has a multilayered meaning here. The most obvious layer allows one to understand the "Other" as the mother, that is, the caretaking person who marks the jouissance of the child via her own signifiers. As noted earlier, this is quite similar to contemporary mentalization and attachment theory (Fonagy et al., 2002), which has empirically demonstrated that a child gets access to its own arousal only via the mirroring of the primary caretaker. A second meaning is more complex: as discussed earlier, the "Other" indicates one's own body as an organism as well. This is the essentially other part of ourselves that will remain other—as in the classic gap between psyche and soma, and whose burps (see Lacan's invasions) require time and again a psychological processing.

ited, presumably by the father, and punishable by castration. This *imaginary* castration covers up and conceals a fundamental truth, namely that enjoyment is impossible from the moment that one speaks. This is the *symbolic* castration, as a given of structure.

With this theory, Lacan takes his leave both from Freud's Oedipus complex and from his own previous conception of it. The authoritarian father prohibiting jouissance, eventually threatening the subject with castration, is nothing but a social neurotic construction on top of an a priori given: the impossibility of jouissance. As a construction, it belongs to the Imaginary order, including the dreamt-of possibility of a final totality, be it in matters of identity or jouissance. In opposition to this, Lacan considers the Symbolic order as structurally incomplete, and even more fundamentally sees this incompleteness as necessary for the functioning of the system. The fact that he denominates this lack as symbolic *castration* doesn't improve the comprehensibility of his theory.

In this new view of the oedipal structure, the father acts merely as an agent of symbolic castration. The living father can never coincide with the function of the master agency. The agent here is nothing but an executive, "my agent," who is or ought to be paid to do a certain job: that of the master agency (Lacan, 2006 [1969–70], pp. 126, 169). This job amounts to presenting the master signifier, "master" because it provides both an identity for the subject and a safeguarding regulation in matters of enjoyment. The agent's task amounts to this presentation, but what it comes down to is passing on the lack from father to son (ibid., pp. 121–129), because no one is able to keep up the appearance of the master signifier. Accordingly, this agent must be regarded as very far removed from the idea of the almighty primal father. Humility is more appropriate than hubris.

Lacan had already discussed the humiliated father earlier. From his paper on *Les complexes familiaux* (Lacan, 1984 [1938]) down to a discussion of a play by Claudel[18] in Seminar VIII (1991 [1960–61]), the humiliation and degradation of the father was considered as a sign of the decline of society and at the same time as a general cause of psychopathology. With these ideas, Lacan stayed with Freud. At the end of Seminar XVII, we encounter something different. Finally, the position of the father is one of shame. Shame, because he must represent a master signifier in the full consciousness that this is an impossible task. "But perhaps it was simply someone who was ashamed, who put himself forward like that. [. . .] This is perhaps what it really is, the hole from which the master signifier arises" (Lacan, 2006 [1969–70], pp. 188–189). Shame, too, because the father will never be able to fill in the lack: he can only pass it on to the next generation.

Hence the task of the father is quite paradoxical. He has to represent the full authority—the "master agency"—knowing that such an authority is an illusion. This is without any doubt the most difficult part of the father role, one that has reached a new peak in our contemporary society. During patriarchal times, every father automatically had authority, based upon an implicit association to the super patriarch, be it a primal father or a father-god. Today, the omnipresent awareness of a structurally determined failure in any authority has made it virtually impossible

[18] Paul Claudel, a famous French writer, published *Le Père humilié* (The Humiliated Father) in 1909, as the last part of his trilogy on the Coûfontaine family.

for many young fathers to take this position, even if only for a minute. What Lacan tells us, however, is that a child needs the father's authority for its identity formation, and that it is the task of the father to *represent* this master agency, along with the passing on of the lack.

Ultimately, for Lacan father and child join forces: the child is the father of the man, as it obliges him to take this position. As the agent of the master agency, the father is confronted with his own impotence from the moment that he speaks and makes a demand—especially because of his dependence on woman for his satisfaction. And the infant itself starts with an original impotence and helplessness. It is clear that we are a long way from the exclusive signifier of the Name-of-the-Father. Good-bye *pater potestas patris familias*.

In the meantime, it has become more and more obvious that identity acquisition and the regulation of jouissance are two sides of the same coin—the oedipal coin, that is. Indeed, both of them come from the Other, and more particularly from the signifiers presented by the others. Until now I have focused on how, in this new theory, the invasions of jouissance are regulated via the Other. But even at the time of Lacan's mirror stage theory, drive regulation and identity acquisition went hand in hand. The first layer of the "*Je*" (the I), the body scheme, comes from the Other and is wrapped around the component drives. In his last theory, jouissance is regulated via the signifiers coming from the Other—and these are the very same signifiers through which the subject acquires its identity. This brings us to our final topic, the regulation of jouissance as subject formation.

identity

Introduction

What function does the oedipal structure serve in human development? The answer that can be distilled from both Freud and Lacan, and that the more empirical investigations of attachment and mentalization theory seem to confirm, is that the oedipal structure has everything to do with identity formation and drive regulation. It is becoming increasingly clear that these are two sides of the same coin.

These three theories begin with a similar premise: identity

is not innate or inborn. This has far-reaching ontological implications, since it means that there is no such thing as an original and authentic self. The newborn baby does not arrive filled with original content. Rather, the neonate finds itself in a state of helplessness, with no idea or image of what it is. Of course a number of genetic potentialities lie waiting that will be realized interactively as the infant develops. The infant's motive is survival in a context of confrontation with "arousal"—which we could describe as the confrontation with undifferentiated drive tensions that arise somatically from inside the baby's own body. For Freud, the initial drives will be grafted onto the infant's instinctual reactions via the nursing situation. In part because they don't imply a gender differentiation, these initial drives are referred to as the "component" or "pregenital" drives. In his reading a drive literally does drive the human being. Hence Freud's most beautiful definition: "a drive is without quality, and, so far as mental life is concerned, is only to be regarded as a measure of the demand made upon the mind for work" (Freud, 1978 [1905d], p. 168), to which he added in 1915: "in consequence of its connection with the body" (1978 [1915c], p. 122).

The primary reactions to such an arousal follow a pattern that is essentially the same. The helpless baby turns to the other by crying. The other is supposed to take care of the "specific actions" that will relieve the inner tension, in a performative and in a symbolic way (Freud, 1978 [1895]). I call them performative and symbolic because such interventions usually combine caretaking acts with words, communicating to the child that the other has understood the demand and is trying to respond to it. At the same time, the other presents a psychic translation of what the child experiences.

As a consequence it is from the very beginning of development that the other takes on a great deal of responsibility for regulating one's own drive arousal—without this other, things would go awry. While answering, the other needs to interpret what is going on inside the baby. And inevitably the fears and desires of this other will play an important role in the way she or he helps the infant regulate its affect. From the Lacanian point of view we would say that while caring for the infant the (m)Other marks her jouissance on the body of the child. In other words, the early experiences of caregiving that are so much the focus of attachment theory and developmental research are in Lacanian terms also at the very same time experiences of the Other's desire. As Lacan has most aptly stated, "Man's desire is the desire of the Other" (Lacan, 1994 [1964], p. 235). Freud's hypothesis of the mother as a "seductress" makes a kind of sense when viewed through this lens.

This psychological *expression* of the other becomes an *impression* for the infant. Through the other's reactions, the child acquires mental access to what it experiences in the real of its body while learning a first way to handle it as well. During moments of pleasure or unpleasure, the parent combines his or her mirroring with a "how do I handle this" message. To paraphrase Lacan, we can say that it is not only the unconscious that is the discourse of the Other, but indeed the conscious as well. It is here that we find the basis of our identity.

Identitas *and separation anxiety*

Today it is more or less generally accepted that as children we identify with the mirroring reactions of the other and thereby acquire an identity of our "own." Despite the discovery of the so-called mirror neurons, how this identification works is not yet clear. A similar process was originally described by Freud in terms of incorporation and introjection, when he was discussing the idea of negation (Freud, 1978 [1925h]). Lacan's theory of the mirror stage and subject formation provides a further elaboration. Developmental psychology and attachment theory are reframing the investigation, and the surprising conclusion is that *our* identity comes from *the other.*

In the Lacanian approach, the accent has to a great degree been put on the idea of alienation, following the words of the poet Rimbaud "I is another" (*Je est un autre*). There is no original identity in the infant itself; but, under normal circumstances, an external identity awaits, embedded in the personal history of the father and the mother, and often revealed first of all in the infant's given name, which is almost never neutral. For Lacan, the mirror presented by the Other reflects much more than the infant's arousal; it reflects as well what he calls the discourse of the Other, meaning that the Other's history will be fully present in it. Human identity is constructed by way of identification with the signifiers of the desire of the other. Stressing this impact of the other on identity, Lacan refers to this process as *alienation.*

Yet in focusing so strongly on this structurally determined alienation, the Lacanian approach tends to ignore that such mirroring may or may not correspond to what the child is experiencing in its own body and that the child always brings a kind of drive regulation. Indeed, the mirror stage installs a kind of bodily identity as well, through which the component drives first become ordered. It is through this shift that the role distribution and social "cunning" described by Lacan will become possible.

In mentalization theory (Fonagy et al., 2002), the alienating aspects receive less attention and the focus is on the correspondence between the other's mirroring, the actual arousal of the infant, and on the affect regulation that results. What the infant receives from the other is not just a mirroring interpretation of what is going on in the child; it also contains indications of ways to handle it. The other demonstrates and tells us what we feel, why we have that feeling, and how to cope with it. Inevitably, during this process the other will impose his or her own "Sense and Sensibility." Identity is nothing other than the development of a representational construction which comes from the other and that provides us with a regulatory access to our own drive life, right from the very moment of birth.[1]

What this means is that we have to take the word "identity" literally. It comes from the Latin *identitas*, meaning similarity. The infant wants to be as similar as possible to what it is mirrored by. Contemporary developmental psychological

---

[1] In this sense, a remark often heard during clinical practice (mostly coming from hysterical patients) is correct: "I'm not original, I am a fake," and so on. To which we have to add that this goes for everyone. The idea of an independent authentic personality, independent of the desire of the other, is an (especially obsessional-neurotic) illusion.

research has demonstrated that during the first three months babies are almost exclusively oriented toward contingency with what the other produces. That is, they want to join the mirroring.[2] In this way, identity acquisition is a process of normalization: we adopt the norm of the other, and hence of the Other, thereby becoming normal.

This original orientation toward contingency comes with a tendency to move toward a close relationship with the other. The infant needs the other on an elemental, evolutionarily determined level. Such an orientation toward contingency—toward converging with the images presented to one—can be read as an expression of Freud's Eros or life drive. According to his definition, the most important feature of Eros is a tendency toward unification, binding together different elements (Freud, 1978 [1940a], p. 148). All of this, however, in line with Lacan's thought, means that a correction to Freud is needed, because the most important primal anxiety is not castration

[2] This first identity is fairly elementary in the sense that it has a dual character. The same goes for psychic functioning in that period. Two-year-olds recognize themselves in the mirror through a relation of equivalence, but they are unable to distinguish between present and earlier images. This is connected to the dualistic functioning of that period, which developmental psychology calls the "psychic equivalence mode": the subject's thoughts and reality are the same, there's no awareness of a difference between representation and external reality (Fonagy et al., 2002, p. 258ff; Verhaeghe, 2004, pp. 166–169). At that same age, we find the complete reverse as well, the "pretend mode": the child's make-believe play is completely separated from reality, and it will make this quite clear. Should the play become too "real"—usually because of an intervention by an adult who wants to play along—the result is anxiety (Fonagy et al., 2002, pp. 261–263). In short, in the equivalence mode reality and thought completely coincide; in the pretend mode, they are completely apart. The integration of these two modes is finally established at the age of four, when children are capable of making a distinction between internal and external reality. This transition is what the oedipal period is concerned with.

anxiety, but *separation anxiety*. The absence of the other is the most dreaded situation, and that is precisely why the child has every reason to follow the mirroring of the other as closely as possible, and initially the other's desire as well, as it is included in these reflections. Later, and precisely because of further oedipal development, the original separation anxiety may shift toward an anxiety about not sufficiently meeting the image as expected by the other—that is, of not adequately answering the desire of the other. The moment this desire of the other is translated in phallic terms, the idea of castration anxiety is not far away. Underneath, though, separation anxiety remains central.

However, in regard to matters of identity development and drive regulation, the focus of contemporary infant research and attachment theory is quite different compared to the views of Freud and Lacan. Indeed, one focus of attachment and mentalization study is on the mother, often camouflaged today in politically correct terms as "the primary caretaker." The infant's primary relationship with the mother is of the utmost importance for the development of identity, and for that matter for development altogether. Contemporary clinical research demonstrates time and again that a so-called safe attachment provides a firm base for later psychological well-being. Freud only later on gives recognition in his theory to the importance of the mother, and even then she will never be given the same weight as the father. And while Lacan situates the primary source of identity in the mother via the mirror stage, he describes this stage as imbued with the negativity of alienation. Thus, when Lacan introduces the idea of a first Other and a second Other, the accent again is clearly on the second one, or the father.[3] Moreover, in much of his theory, a threat is seen to arise from motherly desire and enjoyment of the child. Thus we encounter once again the opposition mentioned in our Introduction, in which both Freud and Lacan privilege the father while neglecting—or even branding as dangerous—the mother who is at the center of the post-Freudian Anglo-Saxon approach.

Perhaps the explanation for these differences may not be too difficult. Anglo-Saxon psychoanalysis developed very much in tandem with child analysis and has a long tradition of highly developed infant-observation techniques, employed both in cases of normal and pathological development. Freud and Lacan, on the other hand, worked exclusively with adult patients who had presumably lived through their own pathological development—otherwise they wouldn't have been patients. Consequently Freud and Lacan will have chiefly met the retroactive effects of an unsafe attachment in combination with a negative or even an almost absent mother image in their clinical practice. (We leave the hypothesis that both Freud and Lacan had a peculiar attachment to their own mother as fodder for the *hystoro*graphs.) In any case, the child's primary relationship to the (m)Other in what is known as the pre-oedipal phase has to be seen as integral to the oedipal structure. Without the pre-oedipal phase, the oedipal structure wouldn't make much sense.

---

[3] Again, these concepts are multilayered. The first Other indicates both the primary caretaker and the body, and that's why Lacan talks about "the Other of the body" as well; the second Other indicates both the father and the Law, hence the synonymous "the Other of the law."

Difference and fusion anxiety

Identity formation cannot be driven exclusively by a desire to converge with the presented mirroring. If it were, the world would be full of clones. Beyond the tendency we've seen for union and identification, there must be a process that permits us to take our distance from the presented images—and hence from the other. And that is exactly what is provided by Freud's other fundamental drive, the death drive, with its propensity to undo connections (Freud, 1978 [1940a], p. 148). Here, the post-Freudian literature talks about individuation and separation (Mahler, Pine, and Bergman, 1975).

Yet, strangely enough, this need for distance, a move away from connectedness, is not much acknowledged in our three theories of identity formation. In Freud it is lacking altogether. Lacan describes alienation and separation as the two processes in subject formation, but his focus is on the first one. In the work of Fonagy and colleagues (Fonagy et al., 2002), separation passes almost unnoticed. And yet, separation can be considered to be the final goal of the oedipal period. As a process, it has to do with an extension and a limitation. Extension, because, as in Lacan, the first Other is complemented with the second Other. Limitation, because the previously unrelated component drives are now subsumed under the phallic heading.[4] As we will see,

---

[4] Indeed, Freud's component or partial drives are initially components of nothing; it seems as if they function independently. It is only after the installation of genital dominance that they retroactively acquire a phallic meaning (see oral and anal phallic) and truly become "component" drives.

both the extension and the limitation apply to identity acquisition and drive regulation.

Extension coincides with a developmental rise in cognitive possibilities. Of course, the second Other was there in the beginning as well, but it is not that clear whether it is possible for the infant to perceive different others as different entities. From a certain point in development, this capacity becomes obvious. The child does not just see itself through the eyes of the first Other; it can see itself via the gaze of the second Other as well. Moreover, it now has the capacity to perceive the first Other through the eyes of the second Other and vice versa. Time and again the images thus represented provide different possibilities for identification, possibilities that will never overlap or may even move further apart. When the dimension of difference arises, it includes all the differences between the child, the first Other, and the second Other, as well as the difference between the two genders and the difference between the two generations.

It would be possible to present this process purely in cognitive and developmental psychological terms, based upon ample contemporary research. But once we consider identity acquisition in terms of gender identity we are in the realm of the psychoanalytic. The transition from infant to boy or girl is anything but easy to understand and, as far as I know, developmental psychology and infant research and mentalization theory do not present clear answers in this respect. It is here that I want to understand the oedipal structure as a triangulation that permits the subject to leave the original dualistic relationships and to position itself between different others that have different desires. It results in what today is called the reflective capacity—

that is, the competence to look both at oneself and at another from something that we can only call a "third position," a position "outside" oneself.

In this way a possibility for a new choice is opened, one beyond the determinative effects of the alienating pre-oedipal experience of mirroring. Who am I, in relation to the desire of the first Other? Who am I in relation to the desire of the second Other? What place do I take in between those two? The answers to those questions imply two important positions. First there is the gender position, to be understood as: How do I relate to the sexualized desire of the Other? Next, there is the generational position: How do I relate to authority? Both these positions entail an identity and a drive regulation. Gender identity as presented by an Orthodox Jewish Other will be different and imply different regulations when compared to the mirroring presented by a postmodern Other. Yet different as these might be, they are, structurally, the result of the same process. In further differentiation, Freud already indicated that from a certain period onward the pregenital drives become bundled under the phallic flag, without losing their specific character because of it. Within Lacanian theory, the differential element becomes the fourth term of the oedipal triangle: the symbolic phallus.

Today, presenting the phallus as the differentiating element is "not done" in many intellectual circles because it doesn't fit their ideology. Irrespective of the latter, the fact remains that most children will define the gender difference in terms of the presence or absence of a penis. The explanation is probably quite simple: it is the most visible distinction. But penis does not equal phallus. As we will see, Lacan's understanding of the phallus is quite different from Freud's penis envy theory. The focus on the phallus in Lacan does not change anything in the motivation for identity acquisition: the subject still needs to find an answer for its own drive arousal. Within the dualistic relationship, this comes down to identifying with the desire of the other. At this point, Lacan posits a precept quite foreign to mentalization and attachment theory: that every identification occurs on the basis of a structurally determined impossibility and lack. Whatever the accuracy of the mirroring representations of the Other may be, by their very nature as representations they will inevitably fall short in truly expressing the child's experience. That is, the other's mirroring representations will never be able to fully cover the gap between the real and the drive underneath, for the same reason that a word can never fully represent a thing. Moreover, it is precisely because they are representations that they will brand the child's own experience of itself and its body with an inherent lack and impossibility. This is what Lacan meant by his statement that the signifier is not only the means to rediscover jouissance: it is also the cause of its loss.

Consequently, every answer by the Other is insufficient, something that Freud already described when he said that it seemed as if our children are forever unsatisfied (Freud, 1978 [1931b], p. 234). The reverse is true as well; the child too does not produce a totally satisfactory answer to the desire of the Other, and as a result neither mother nor child can fulfill their respective desires. The impossibility of finding a definitive answer in the first Other is the impetus for a shift toward the second Other in order to find "the" answer there. This impetus will only be strengthened when the child observes that the first

Other does not limit her desire to the child, but desires something from the second Other (traditionally the father) as well.

The assumption that the father has got "it" implies the installation of a mediatory point between mother and child. What this "it" constitutes is far from clear for the child. And the same lack of clarity lingers on in adults. Think of expressions like "That woman really *has something*!" or "That guy's *got it*." The moment this "something" or "it" must be defined, we brush up against an impossibility. The sole thing to emerge is that "it" has something to do with sex and gender, and that it is supposed to answer our desire for an answer from the Other—or to answer the question of what we should give to the Other in order to obtain jouissance.

Freud's interpretation is as radical as it is naive: "it" is the real penis. Lacan abstracts it and dubs it the phallus. The real penis can leave us with the illusion that desire, even the drive itself, can be satisfied. The phallus, in contrast, is a signifier and in that sense only an indicator of the dreamt-of, unreachable endpoint of desire, the signifier for what would finally resolve the lack and do the job. The second Other, traditionally embodied by the father, is only presumed to possess this phallus, nothing more.

To the extent that this phallus is reduced to the Imaginary order, the illusion remains in place that there can be a conclusive answer to desire via imaginary identification. Such an illusion inevitably leads to *Guinness Book of Records* hysteria in men and to "Miss World" hysteria in women. What is typical in this regard is that the subject's functioning remains on a dualistic level despite the presence of three or more characters. It is at this point that we can truly situate the Oedipus complex as a *complex* of rivalry combined with castration anxiety. This rivalry sustains a dualistic logic where there is a choice of either me or the other, and thus points to the fact that the oedipal situation has not been worked through symbolically.

In such a case, desire demands that it be answered fully and exclusively, either by the other for me or by me for the other. Psychopathology—including everyday psychopathology—demonstrates a number of well-known variants. "I have/am the phallus more (or less) than that other" (competition). "The other doesn't give me enough of the phallus" (revendication). "Not I but that other has/is the phallus" (jealousy). "I don't have/I'm not the phallus and will never have/be it" (depression). "I have/am the phallus" (narcissism). Within such dualistic logic, the subject wants to take the first and exclusive position with the other, especially when in comparison with yet another other. The protagonists of such an everyday tragicomedy can be quite different, as can their respective positions, but the underlying structure will always be the same.

Thus considered, a threesome doesn't necessarily imply triangularity, since within a threesome the actual relationship(s) may remain dualistic. The variants described above demonstrate how the original separation anxiety is rewritten in phallic terms and even becomes castration anxiety: I will be left by the other if I don't have the phallus enough. While less expected from a Freudian point of view, the reverse is also quite possible—that is, the anxiety of having to meet the desire of the other far too much, without there being any space left for oneself. This is the anxiety that is almost constantly present in Lacan's descriptions of the mother–child relationship. While Freud barely mentions this kind of anxiety it corresponds to attachment theory's resistant-avoidant attachment (Mahler et al., 1975), which forms in reaction to the preoccupied parent. In contrast to separation anxiety, here we find the other side, namely *fusion anxiety* (sometimes called intrusion anxiety), in combination with a desire for autonomy. These names express only weakly the implicit threat that is dreaded from a supposedly big, devouring other—what I have called the crocodile effect.

Although Freud does not discuss this anxiety, I have described the way his theory presents a solution to it, neurotic though it may be. I am referring to his creation of the primal father whose task it is to fulfill the desire of the mother, or even of all women, thus taking away their potential threat. With its paternal metaphor, Lacan's first oedipal theory too emphasizes that the father's function is to separate mother and child. However, based on attachment theory and on Lacan's last theory, we can say that the underlying danger originally has nothing to do with the other, and has everything to do with one's own drive. The anxiety at being overwhelmed by something internal is easier to handle once it is projected to the outside world, in this case, onto the other.

A failure in separation indicates that the oedipal structure is not fully installed. Consequently, relations will continue on a dualistic level, and thus truly give rise to an Oedipus complex. As the classical Freudian version would have it, the other will seem too big (as in "the primal father has the phallus, I don't have it or don't have enough of it") and a competing and demanding relationship will be installed. Within a classic Lacanian version, the other is not big enough and he needs support. In the Freudian complex, the other has to be pulled down constantly, in the Lacanian version he has to be buttressed all the time. In both cases, it remains a fight on an imaginary battlefield with an immediate profit to be had, one that is gained by allowing the subject to face its own drive outside itself via someone else.

From dualistic-imaginary to triangular-symbolic

In a dualistic relationship there are typically only two alternatives, either to coincide or to separate. The way these terms can be reversed and exchanged gives an indication of the way an Oedipus complex can go in either of two directions. Mothers who fear to be gobbled up by their children, fathers who compete with their sons are anything but exceptions. Indeed, dualistic relationships make every position reversible, a possibility that received hardly any attention from Freud. For Lacan, it is a core characteristic of the Imaginary order.

Within a triangular relationship as described by Lacan the phallus functions as a signifier, and the structural presence of a lack in the relationship between a child and his parents is recognized. This opening then makes it possible for the subject-to-be to realize something on its own in an elsewhere with someone else. This is the meaning of the incest prohibition and the obligation for exogamy: the child must evolve from a dualistic relationship and has to make later and elsewhere a choice to create something, namely an identity of its own in relation both to the Other and to its own drive. If this succeeds, the oedipal structure has carried out its function. The drive-regulating aspect will again appear under the form of an identification, this time a symbolic one. With an imaginary identification the difference is that it is then possible to take one's distance and to consciously consider different choices.

Of course this does not mean that there is a complete solution to the problem of the drive and its regulation. That would be contrary to Lacan's idea about the lack in the Symbolic order and the not-all. The usual way of coping with this impossibility was already described by Freud: it is symptom formation. Lacan generalizes this idea. There is no subject without a symptom because that is the only way to handle the impossibility of jouissance. As we will see in our next chapter, at the end of his work Lacan introduces the idea of "the sinthome" as a solution that is consciously chosen and/or constructed by a subject. In contrast to the unconsciously determined symptom, this solution has to do with what he calls a real identification.

For Freud, the normal solution comes via the oedipal symbolic identification with the father, resulting in the formation of the superego and the paternal prohibition. How are we to read this prohibition? For Freud, it is the prohibition against incest, and it is aimed in particular at the child. But Lacan imposes the prohibition on the mother. Until his last theory, that is, when he will finally understand this prohibition as the social styling of an a priori, given impossibility, as described above: total jouissance is impossible for the living because it would entail death. Whatever the apodictic nature of this idea, it fits a certain familiar experience. Because, in fact, the human subject never goes all the way in matters of jouissance—there seems to be a kind of internal brake system (Freud, 1978 [1892–99],

p. 222). Social styling may produce a particular distribution of gender roles between the parents, but for Lacan this is indeed only a styling of an impossibility that was already there. Thus the responsibility for one's own jouissance and one's own drive is shifted toward the woman–mother while the responsibility for the safeguarding prohibition is put on the shoulders of the man–father.

What actual role the father plays in the oedipal situation can get lost in all of this. The contemporary political correctness isn't of much help either, as it forbids anything that reminds one of a "patriarchal bias," often with caricatured effects. Today, any discussion of the paternal may invite accusations of patriarchal bias, sometimes to the point of skewing consideration away from the father at all. It is quite remarkable—to say the least—that an entire issue of the *Psychoanalytic Quarterly* on "The Third in Psychoanalysis" contains only one paper (Britton, 2004) that refers to the Oedipus complex! Even in Lacan's theory there is a decline in the importance attributed to the father figure. Obviously, the introduction of a third mediating point is not necessarily connected to one particular figure, let alone exclusively linked to the father.

Even more forgotten is the dimension of prohibition. In Freud's classic theory it is the father who forbids the child to enjoy the mother. In Lacan's first interpretation, it is the mother who is forbidden to enjoy her child. In his last theory, he indicates how this prohibition is the product of a social construction; in fact it is only a camouflaged replacement of something far more fundamental, namely the impossibility of jouissance in itself. Within infant research and attachment theory, the focus is on the regulating character of the mirroring, the idea of prohibition being implicitly present in the very idea of regulation.

Prohibition would seem to be necessary to each of these theories, despite their differences. Yet in postmodern thinking the idea of prohibition has almost disappeared, probably because any form of power within a relationship has become suspect. Following Lacan's last reasoning, a progressive disappearance of prohibition will result in a paradoxical effect. Jouissance will not become more easily available, and not only because jouissance in itself is impossible, but because anxiety will increase, especially the neurotic anxiety of being overwhelmed because of the lack of a safeguard. Another prediction is easy to make as well: because of this increasing anxiety, the social cunning machine will evoke a contrary movement that will preach prohibition in an unnuanced form. Based upon Freud's theory it is predictable that such a movement will advocate a return to the supposed safety of the primal father and that the accompanying aggression will be directed against the other. Based upon Lacan's theory we can predict that women will be thrust into the role of this other. The contemporary return to ultra right-wing conservatism in combination with Christian–Jewish–Muslim fundamentalism might serve as a paradigmatic example. Salvation is yet again expected from an almighty savior.

By way of conclusion, I can summarize the oedipal structure as follows. The starting point is a confrontation with the jouissance arising from one's own body, a demand against which the infant does not initially have its own form of defense. Appealing to the Other results in an answer upon which a first layer of identity and a first drive regulation, adopted from the first Other (i.e., an other and his or her mirroring), are based. In this way the threat coming from one's own drive becomes externally manageable via that Other. The price that must be paid is an obligatory identification with the Other's desire, even if this puts one at risk of totally disappearing in the first Other and only being allowed to exist as a kind of appendage. Things change considerably once a second Other is recognized as a supposed owner of the answer to desire, which in the meantime has been translated into phallic terms. This opens the possibility for the subject to take a position of its own. The central matter here is not just the transition from the dual to the triangular via the introduction of a third point, but—especially—the recognition of a structurally determined lack. With that, shifting and choosing in matters of identification and desire become possible.

Changes in contemporary society confront us with a number of questions. The existence of both social cunning and the ensuing role distribution described by Lacan seem inevitable. Jouissance needs to be located in a first other, meaning that the prohibition will be directed against this first other as well. Traditionally, the first other is incarnated by the mother and the second other by the father. Contemporary clinical practice demonstrates that such a role distribution is not a necessity. It is far from clear that this second other has to be a concrete person at all, let alone a father and some contemporary theories talk about the importance of "the Third" or even "Thirdness." In any case, there is enough evidence for the fact that a classic family with a father present can cause as much psychopathology as a nonclassic one. Today there are several conceivable casting schemes, each of which—including the traditional one—will have its own special effects. It is obvious that a single-parent family, a newly composed family, or a homosexual family will each have their own effects on the children they raise. The question is how and in what way the underlying structure and social cunning will make their appearance within these different forms of families.

conclusion: the sinthome

In 1924 Freud published *The Dissolution of the Oedipus Complex*, describing what he considered the necessary destruction of this "central phenomenon of the sexual period of early childhood" (Freud, 1978 [1924d], p. 173). Here, the oedipal wishes are what need to be destroyed. And indeed it is destruction that is required, not repression, which would only result in pathogenic effects (ibid., p. 177). When his experience taught him that instances of such destruction are quite rare, in 1937 he had to conclude that psychoanalytical practice meets a biological bedrock of castration anxiety in men and penis envy in women (Freud, 1978 [1937c]). This brings us to our final theme: if the Oedipus complex cannot be destroyed as it should be (Freud), and if the oedipal structure is a necessary styling of the impossibility of jouissance (Lacan), how then can jouissance be handled?

The responses in Lacan's theory make it much more interesting than Freud's biological deadlock. In Lacan's reading, the Oedipus complex hides a necessary structure that permits the subject to cope with the drives and especially with the jouissance arising from his or her own body. The impossibility of jouissance is transformed into a prohibition, resulting in endless desire and in symptom formation. The Oedipus complex *in itself* is a symptom, meaning that it is an imaginary construction around the real of the drive via the Other. Every particular neurotic symptom is nothing but a particular formation of the Oedipus complex. That is why Freud is correct to point out that every symptom is a form of satisfaction. What Lacan now adds is the inevitability of the symptom: in matters of sexuality, desire, and enjoyment, there is no subject without a symptom.

That is also why the aim of a psychoanalytic practice is not to help someone get rid of his or her symptoms in order to find the right satisfaction. The aim is to install a different kind of symptom on top of the impossibility of jouissance. Instead of Freud's endpoint of the Oedipus complex—the identification with the father—Lacan promotes the *identification with the symptom* as the final goal of his psychoanalytical practice. This permits him to contrast the oedipal solution with what he calls a solution in the Real (see Verhaeghe and Declercq, 2002).

Believing in one's symptom

The meaning of the formula—to identify with one's symptom—may be understood by comparing it with its usual alternative: to believe in one's symptom. What the symptom's existence grants is a guarantee that the Other has no lack. Hence, such a belief in the symptom implies a belief in the Other of the Other, namely in the primal father and the guarantee he is supposed to provide. This condition is typical at the beginning of an analysis. The patient comes to the analyst because she or he is convinced—and rightly so—that his or her symptom has a meaning. In this way the analyst is put in the position of the one who knows, the one who will reveal this hidden signification, the Other without any lack. To put it differently, the patient lets his symptom be followed by an ellipsis, hoping that it, and others, will receive a final meaning during the analysis, based on the interpretations of the master (Lacan, 1975, p. 109). This meaning is supposed to open the road to a final satisfactory life in which The Sexual Relationship is realized.

As Freud himself had already experienced, analytic work is effective only up to a certain point. His metaphor in this respect is quite revealing, as he compared symptom formation to what the oyster does: the grain of sand is the root drive around which a pearl is formed, in order to get rid of the irritation (Freud, 1978 [1905e], p. 83). The analytic work may succeed in deconstructing the imaginary signifying layers (the pearl) but this does not mean that the patient gets rid of the original drive component (the grain of sand). On the contrary, the confrontation with the underlying real part of the drive usually entails a confrontation with the lack of the Other as well; and in this respect there is no final answer.

At this crossroads, the analysand has two possible choices. Either she or he sticks to the classic solution and looks for yet another meaning by way of another hysterical identification with a new guaranteeing Other, or she or he chooses a new solution and identifies with the Real of the symptom.

Such an identification with the symptom is not a matter of finally surrendering. On the contrary, such a surrender characterizes the attitude of belief in the symptom. The neurotic subject considers his or her failure to be an individual fault and remains convinced that other people (that the Other) succeed in realizing The Sexual Relationship. This is not the case for the subject who has identified him/herself with his or her symptom because now the subject has discovered that the failure of the sexual relationship is not a matter of individual impotence but is a structural impossibility.

The discovery of this choice implies a change in the subject's position with regard to jouissance. Before, the subject situated all jouissance on the side of the Other (Freud's primal father, Lacan's crocodile mother); after undergoing this change, the subject situates the jouissance in the Real of his or her own body. Hence, there is no longer a jouissance prescribed by the Other. For Lacan, this identification with the symptom results in what he has called the *sinthome*. With this equivocal neologism, he covers at least three different signifiers: "*symptôme*" (symptom), *saint homme* (holy man), and Saint Thomas (the apostle who did not believe the Other—Christ—and went for the real thing, putting his finger in the wound).

This is the choice we have: either a symptom or a sinthome.

Creatio ex nihilo: *The sinthome*

The normal symptom is the social symptom, in which one follows the norm of the Other. Every society has created institutions through which the impossibility of jouissance may be handled, endorsing these by rituals and tokens and embedding them in symbolic systems of belief, from religion to science. Sooner or later, every subject discovers the failure of these institutions and has to look for other answers. More often than not, and in spite of the usual hysterical protests, he or she remains within the system—that is, within the belief that a correct answer is guaranteed by an Other without a lack—and constructs a number of private symptoms while looking for a new Other. This search is usually accompanied by the search for a new concrete other as well, as the blame for the failure may very well be put on the previous partner. Its repetitive reiteration may lead the subject either to frustrated submission or to the creation of a new kind of symptom.

What is essential for such a creation is that the subject has freed himself of the Other. This is probably what Kazantzakis meant in his *Report to Greco*—at the end of his spiritual search: the most important salvation is the salvation from the very idea of salvation (Kazantzakis, 1973). To be sure, it is a fiction, but it is a fiction that does not turn the subject into a dupe since she or he has created it by him- or herself. By the end of Seminar XX, during which Lacan explained why the subject has to fall back on an endless "encore" precisely because of the impossibility of jouissance, he had already evoked this creation of a new signifier in talking about poetry. Here, creation is only creation when it builds on the lack of the Other—that is, insofar as it is a *creatio ex nihilo*.

Lacan calls this self-created fiction a *sinthome*: a particular signifier that knots the three registers of the Real, the Symbolic, and the Imaginary into a particular sexual rapport: "On the level of the *sinthome*, there is a relationship. There is only a relationship where there is a *sinthome*" (Lacan, 1977 [1976], p. 20; 1977, pp. 5–7). Accordingly, this creation permits a completely new approach to the question of gender. Both man and woman are locked up in the alienating role distribution dictated by the cunning Other and his ever-phallic signifiers. Instead of being reduced to an ever-failing categorization (men versus women) and the related impossible relation between them, the emphasis is now on difference. It is no coincidence that in the best of cases lovers invent a new language of their own, usually beginning with a new name for each other.

What can we conclude from these thoughts on neurosis and on the conclusion of a psychoanalytic cure? I hope to have made it clear that normally, that is, neurotically, jouissance is identified with the mother, forbidden by the father, and expected to be found elsewhere later. But this never happens as completely as expected. Moreover, destroying the prohibition does not open the road to jouissance, but just the reverse. Symptom formation provides substitute satisfactions without really changing anything. Exchanging private symptoms for social symptoms may result in a kind of normalization, but this will be at the expense of the subject. The aim of the creation of a *sinthome* is to be able to function without a guaranteeing Other. That's why the ultimate goal of analysis is absolute difference: "There only may the signification of a limitless love emerge, because it is outside the limits of the law, where alone it may live" (Lacan, 1994 [1964], p. 276).

bibliography

ANDRÉ, S. (2000). *What Does a Woman Want?* New York: Other Press.

BENJAMIN, J. (2004). Beyond doer and done to: an intersubjective view of Thirdness. *Psychoanalytic Quarterly* 1: 5–46.

BRITTON, R. (2004). Subjectivity, objectivity, and triangular space. *Psychoanalytic Quarterly* 1: 47–62.

CHODOROW, N. (1999). *The Reproduction of Mothering: Psychoanalysis and the Sociology of Gender*. 2nd ed. Berkeley, CA: University of California Press.

ELLENBERGER, H. F. (1970). *On the Discovery of the Unconscious: The History and Evolution of Dynamic Psychiatry*. New York: Basic Books.

FONAGY, P., GERGELY, G., JURIST, E., AND TARGET, M. (2002). *Affect*

Regulation, Mentalization, and the Development of the Self. New York: Other Press.

FREUD, S. (1978 [1892–99]). *Extracts from the Fliess Papers. The Standard Edition of the Complete Psychological Works of Sigmund Freud*, Vol. 1, pp. 175–280. London: Hogarth Press.

———. (1978 [1895]). *A Project for a Scientific Psychology. Standard Edition*, Vol. 1, pp. 281–397. London: Hogarth Press.

———. (1978 [1896]). *Draft K. Standard Edition*, Vol. 1, pp. 220–229. London: Hogarth Press.

———. (1978 [1900a]). *The Interpretation of Dreams. Standard Edition*, Vols. 4–5. London: Hogarth Press.

———. (1978 [1905d]). *Three Essays on the Theory of Sexuality. Standard Edition*, Vol. 7, pp. 123–245. London: Hogarth Press.

———. (1978 [1905e]). *Fragment of an Analysis of a Case of Hysteria. Standard Edition*, Vol. 7, pp. 1–122. London: Hogarth Press.

———. (1978 [1909b]). *Analysis of a Phobia in a Five-Year-Old Boy. Standard Edition*, Vol. 10, pp. 1–149. London: Hogarth Press.

———. (1978 [1909c]). *Family Romances. Standard Edition*, Vol. 9, pp. 235–244. London: Hogarth Press.

———. (1978 [1910d]). *The Future Prospects of Psycho-analytic Therapy. Standard Edition*, Vol. 11, pp. 139–151. London: Hogarth Press.

———. (1978 [1910h]). *A Special Type of Choice of Object Made by Men. Standard Edition*, Vol. 11, pp. 163–175. London: Hogarth Press.

———. (1978 [1910k]). *'Wild' Psycho-analysis. Standard Edition*, Vol. 11, pp. 219–227. London: Hogarth Press.

———. (1978 [1912–13]). *Totem and Taboo. Standard Edition*, Vol. 13, pp. 1–162. London: Hogarth Press.

———. (1978 [1913c]). *On Beginning the Treatment (Further Recommendations on the Technique of Psycho-analysis I). Standard Edition*, Vol. 12, pp. 121–144. London: Hogarth Press.

———. (1978 [1914g]). *Remembering, Repeating and Working-through (Further Recommendations on the Technique of Psycho-analysis II). Standard Edition*, Vol. 12, pp. 147–156. London: Hogarth Press.

———. (1978 [1915c]). *Instincts and Their Vicissitudes. Standard Edition*, Vol. 14, pp. 109–140. London: Hogarth Press.

———. (1978 [1916–17]). *Introductory Lectures on Pycho-analysis, Part III: General Theory of the Neuroses. Standard Edition*, Vol. 16, pp. 13–481. London: Hogarth Press.

———. (1978 [1917a]). *A Difficulty in the Path of Psycho-analysis. Standard Edition*, Vol. 17, pp. 137–144. London: Hogarth Press.

———. (1978 [1918b]). *From the History of an Infantile Neurosis. Standard Edition*, Vol. 17, pp. 1–123. London: Hogarth Press.

———. (1978 [1920g]). *Beyond the Pleasure Principle. Standard Edition*, Vol. 18, pp. 7–64. London: Hogarth Press.

———. (1978 [1923e]). *The Infantile Genital Organization. Standard Edition*, Vol. 19, pp. 141–145. London: Hogarth Press.

———. (1978 [1924d]). *The Dissolution of the Oedipus Complex. Standard Edition*, Vol. 19, pp. 173–182. London: Hogarth Press.

———. (1978 [1925d]). *An Autobiographical Study. Standard Edition*, Vol. 20, pp. 7–74. London: Hogarth Press.

———. (1978 [1925h]). *Negation. Standard Edition*, Vol. 19, pp. 233–239. London: Hogarth Press.

———. (1978 [1925j]). *Some Psychical Consequences of the Anatomical Distinction Between the Sexes. Standard Edition*, Vol. 19, pp. 248–258. London: Hogarth Press.

———. (1978 [1931b]). *Female Sexuality. Standard Edition*, Vol. 21, pp. 221–243. London: Hogarth Press.

———. (1978 [1933a]). *Femininity. Standard Edition*, Vol. 22, pp. 112–135. London: Hogarth Press.

———. (1978 [1937c]). *Analysis Terminable and Interminable. Standard Edition*, Vol. 23, pp. 209–253. London: Hogarth Press.

———. (1978 [1939a (1937–39)]). *Moses and Monotheism. Standard Edition*, Vol. 23, pp.1–137. London: Hogarth Press.

———. (1978 [1940a]). *An Outline of Psycho-analysis. Standard Edition*, Vol. 23, pp. 141–208. London: Hogarth Press.

———. (1985 [1915]). *Übersicht der Übertragungsneurosen (Entwurf der zwölften metapsychologischen Abhandlung von 1915*). Gesammelte Werke. Nachtragsband, pp. 627–651. Frankfurt: S. Fischer Verlag.

FREUD, S., AND BREUER, J. (1978 [1895d]). *Studies on Hysteria. Standard Edition*, Vol. 2. London: Hogarth Press.

GRIGG, R. (1999). *Female Sexuality: The Early Psychoanalytic Controversies*. London: Rebus Press.

JONES, E. (1974). *Sigmund Freud. Life and Work, Vol. III: The Last Phase.* London: Hogarth Press.

KAZANTZAKIS, N. (1973). *Report to Greco*, trans. P. A. Bien. London: Faber and Faber.

LACAN, J. (1975). *R.S.I. Séminaire du 21 janvier 1975* [Seminar of January 21, 1975]. *Ornicar?* 3: 104–110.

———. (1977 [1976]). *Le Séminaire XXIII, Le Sinthome. Ornicar?* 8.

———. (1977). *L'insu que sait de l'une bévue s'aile a mourre: séminaire du 16 novembre 1976. Ornicar?*, 12/13: 5–9.

———. (1984 [1938]). *Les complexes familiaux dans la formation de l'individu* [Family complexes in the formation of the individual]. Paris: Navarin.

———. (1991 [1960–61]). *Le séminaire, livre VIII: Le transfert* [The seminar, book VIII: Transference], ed. J.-A. Miller. Paris: Seuil.

———. (1992 [1959–60]). *The Seminar, Book VII: The Ethics of Psychoanalysis*, ed. J.-A. Miller, trans. D. Porter. New York: Norton.

———. (1993 [1955–56]). *The Seminar, Book III: The Psychoses*, trans. G. Russell. New York: Norton.

———. (1994 [1956–57]). *Le séminaire, livre IV: La relation d'objet* [The Seminar, Book IV: The Object Relation], ed. J.-A. Miller. Paris: Seuil.

———. (1994 [1964]). *The Seminar, Book XI: The Fundamental Concepts of Psycho-Analysis*, trans. A. Sheridan. London: Penguin.

———. (1999 [1972–73]). *The Seminar, Book XX: Encore*, ed. J.-A. Miller, trans. B. Fink. New York: Norton.

———. (2003 [1962–63]). *Le séminaire, livre X: L'angoisse* [The Seminar, Book X: Anxiety], ed. J.-A. Miller. Paris: Seuil.

———. (2006 [1955–56]). On a question preliminary to any possible treatment of psychosis. In *Écrits,* trans. B. Fink, H. Fink, and R. Grigg, pp. 445–448. New York: Norton.

———. (2007 [1969–70]). *The Seminar, Book XVII: The Other Side of Psychoanalysis*. ed. J.-A. Miller, trans. R. Grigg. New York: Norton.

LÉVI-STRAUSS, C. (1969 [1949]). *The Elementary Structures of Kinship*, trans. J. H. Bell, J. R. von Sturmer, and R. Needham. London: Eyre & Spottiswoode.

MAHLER, M., PINE, F., AND BERGMAN, A. (1975). *The Psychological Birth of the Human Infant: Symbiosis and Individuation*. New York: Basic Books.

MITCHELL, J. (1975). *Psychoanalysis and Feminism*. Harmondsworth, UK: Penguin.

———. (2003). *Siblings: Sex and Violence*. Cambridge, UK: Polity Press.

NAOURI, A. (2004). *Les pères et les mères* [The fathers and mothers]. Paris: Odile Jacob.

STRACHEY, J., ED. (1975). Editorial note. *The Standard Edition of the Complete Psychological Works of Sigmund Freud*, Vol. 19, pp. 243–247. London: Hogarth Press.

TORT, M. (2000). Lacan's new gospel. In J. M. Rabaté, *Lacan in America,* pp. 153–187. New York: Other Press.

VERHAEGHE, P. (2000 [1987]). *Does the Woman Exist? From Freud's Hysteric to Lacan's Feminine*. Rev. ed. New York: Other Press.

———. (2001). *Beyond Gender: From Subject to Drive*. New York: Other Press.

———. (2004). *On Being Normal and Other Disorders: A Manual for Clinical Psychologists*. New York: Other Press.

———. (2006). Enjoyment and impossibility: Lacan's revision of the Oedipus complex. In J. Clemens and R. Grigg, eds. *Jacques Lacan and the Other Side of Psychoanalysis*, pp. 29–49. Durham, NC: Duke University Press.

VERHAEGHE, P., DECLERCQ, F. (2002). Lacan's analytical goal: "Le Sinthome" or the feminine way. In L. Thurston ed., *Essays on the Final Lacan: Reinventing the Symptom*, pp. 59–83. New York: Other Press.

index